THE
MONGREL

THE
MONGREL

Angela Patmore

Popular Dogs
London Sydney Auckland Johannesburg

Popular Dogs Publishing Co. Ltd.

An imprint of Century Hutchinson

Brookmount House, 62–65 Chandos Place
Covent Garden, London WC2N 4NW

Century Hutchinson Australia (Pty) Ltd
20 Alfred Street, Milsons Point, Sydney 2061

Century Hutchinson New Zealand Limited
191 Archers Road, PO Box 40–086, Glenfield, Auckland 10

Century Hutchinson South Africa (Pty) Ltd
PO Box 337, Bergvlei 2012, South Africa

First published 1985
Reprinted 1988, 1989

Copyright © Angela Patmore 1985

Set in Baskerville by BookEns, Saffron Walden, Essex
Printed and bound in Great Britain by Mackays of Chatham PLC, Chatham, Kent

Cataloguing in Publication Data

Patmore, Angela
    The mongrel
    1. Dogs
    I. Title
    636.7   SF426

ISBN 0 09 162391 X

Contents

Acknowledgements

The author and publishers would like to thank the following:

Battersea Dogs' Home
  Barbara Graham and the Staff
  William Wadman Taylor MRCVS
Dr Peter Bedford, The Royal Veterinary College
British Union for the Abolition of Vivisection
Jilly Cooper
Tony Cowie MRCVS
Dogs Monthly
Leo Donnellan and the Singing Mongrels
Betty Fincham, Lindsay Roebotham and Bugsy Malone
Michael Foot MP
Professor Michael Fox
Dave Grant MRCVS and Barny
The Guide Dogs for the Blind Association
Philip Hale and Adi
John Haslan, Assistant Press Secretary to the Queen
Hearing Dogs for the Deaf
Nigel Hemming
Herald Holiday Handbooks
Hewitts Farm
  Alex Bruce and Geoff Rolstone
Margaret von Hoensbroech and Mazinga
Linda Humphreys and Kahla
Jeremy Irons and Speed
Jenny Kearney, The Grooming Pad
George MacLeod MRCVS, DVSM
Cherry Mitchell and Bambi

Dr Roger Mugford, Consultant in Animal Behaviour
The National Anti-Vivisection Society
   Brian Gunn, General Secretary
The National Canine Defence League
   Mrs Clarissa Baldwin
Our Dogs
   Vince Hogan
The People's Dispensary for Sick Animals
Dr Heather Pidduck, The Royal Veterinary College
PRO Dogs National Charity
   Lesley Scott Ordish
The Royal Society for the Prevention of Cruelty to Animals
The Society for Companion Animal Studies
   Dr Alan Walker
Ian Smith and Samantha
St Francis Charity for Stray Animals
Dorothy Steves
The Wood Green Animal Shelter
   Mr Graham Fuller

Photographic acknowledgements

The author and publisher would like to thank the following for allowing the use of copyright photographs: Associated Newspapers, Battersea Dogs Home, Jilly Cooper, Michael Fox/The Humane Society of the United States, David Grant, Brian Gunn/National Anti-Vivisection Society, Hearing Dogs for the Deaf, Marc Henrie/National Canine Defence League, Linda Humphreys, Illustrated London News, Manchester Daily Mail, Mary Evans Picture Library, Cherry Mitchell, Dr Roger Mugford, PDSA, Roy Phypers, Press Association, Ann Ronan Picture Library, David Rose, RSPCA, South Croydon Advertiser, Dorothy Steves, The Times, John Wright/Guide Dogs for the Blind Association, Anthony M. Glue.

1
The true dog

Thank you for opening this book. Anyone interested in mongrels is a genuine dog person, for the mongrel is the genuine dog. Evolved from wolf progeny domesticated by our prehistoric ancestors perhaps 50,000 years ago, the mongrel, unlike latter-day breed dogs fashioned by man for particular jobs, has been designed by nature, and for no other purpose than survival of the fittest.

The mongrel is the oldest dog in the world. His feral brothers and sisters – such as the dingo, the New Guinea singing dog and the Indian pariah – are the most primitive of all domestic Canids. Dingoes are the descendants of dogs that were taken by man to Australia from eastern Asia many thousands of years ago. They reverted to the wild and today they are hunted down and killed as pests, although the Aborigines respect them and tame them to track game. The dingoes are closely related to the New Guinea singing dogs and Indian pariahs, semi-domesticated mongrels of various hues who live by their wits, scavenging around villages. 'Pariah' is a Tamil word that has come to mean 'outcast'.

Zoologists and naturalists, unlike the general public, recognize the importance of the feral mongrels. Dr Juliet Jewel of the Museum of Natural History in London: 'They are most interesting relics of the dogs that must have been widespread throughout western and eastern Asia during the prehistoric period and as such they should be conserved.'[1]* Canine historians R. Menzel and R. Menzel: 'The question of the

*The notes can be found at the end of this book, on page 194.

pariah dog is among the most interesting of zoological problems, particularly from the point of view of racial history. We can be quite sure that an examination of the history of the domestic dog in all its aspects would reveal that there is scarcely a single facet that might not be illuminated by research into the problem of the pariah dog.'[2] Biologist Miriam Rothschild, writing of her naturalist uncle Walter, who founded the whole concept of subspecies:

> Dr Jordan recalled that Walter's passionate love of dogs proved somewhat embarrassing on collecting expeditions in the wilds of North Africa, for he insisted on establishing friendly relations with the savage feral curs scavenging round their camp. Curiously enough, the dogs never bared their teeth at Walter, and he was never bitten – the attraction was mutual.[3]

Tring Zoological Museum in Hertfordshire (0442 824181), which houses a collection of old-style pedigrees as well as exhibits of the pariah and dingo, says in notes on the primitive mongrels: 'They probably closely resemble the early dogs whose remains are found in archaeological sites.'

Even after thousands of years of domestication, all dogs retain the ability to become feral – to revert to the wild. The mongrel, because it has generally been a street dog, retains the ability very strongly. Studies of feral mongrels in the United States show that Lady and the Tramp live in derelict buildings and scavenge at dawn and dusk. 'Packs' tend to be temporary, following a bitch on heat; it is easier to forage alone. The odd little group does stick together, like the trio in St Louis, Missouri studied by scientist Michael Fox in the 1970s. The group consisted of a female mongrel, a large mutt with a bad hip, and a German shepherd type who seemed to be the gooseberry, following the other two about. Feral dogs like these three are more scabby, skinny and scared than free-roaming dogs with a home to go to. The trio ranged for up to a mile, scavenging in parks and refuse dumps, chasing squirrels without catching any, and keeping in contact by marking, wagging and looking at one another. 'They avoided people, especially children,' said Fox. Once caught, such dogs are executed in primitive gas and decompression chambers by a society that claims to like dogs and breeds rather a lot of them.

Fox concluded: 'This study underlines the tragic consequences [to the dogs] of irresponsible ownership.'[4]

The most ancient dogs in the world were mongrels. The tombs of the pharaohs reveal a motley lot of all shapes and sizes, depicted in bas-relief. The Egyptians worshipped them all. Cheops' own Abakaru, etched, according to one authority, in 3733 BC, was a rangy, pig-tailed, prick-eared mongrel with a disproportionately small head. He is shown wearing a fashionable high-necked collar and a little grin, although the Kennel Club would soon wipe the smile off his face if he tried to enter a show, as a 'pharaoh hound' or anything else. In Europe, real St Bernards from the Hospice of Bernard de Menthon on the Great St Bernard Pass in the Alps were utterly rejected by Victorian show judges and didn't even win cards. Even though the dogs had reputedly cohabited with de Menthon himself in the tenth century AD, they were thought not nearly so nice as the 'proper' St Bernard pedigrees bred in England, and valued at £10,000 apiece. But we can go back much further than that. The oldest dog fossil found to date, the German *Oberkassel* dog excavated near Bonn and thought to be 14,000 years old, was a mongrel. The Palegawra Cave in Iraq turned up another muttly specimen, also dated to about 14,000 years ago. Another dog fossil, found at the Natufian site in Israel with its owner's skeletal hand resting on its head, is a mongrel pup thought to have been four or five months old when it died 12,000 years ago. British dog skeletons have been unearthed at Windmill Hill and Easton Down in Wiltshire, at Grimes Graves, Norfolk and at Starr Carr, Yorkshire – mongrels all.

In addition to having the longest canine lineage on earth and being the most varied in colour and conformation, the mongrel is also the most widespread. The population worldwide is something in the region of 150 million, flourishing in every human habitat, withstanding extremes of climate and terrain, horror and hardship, as well as the cruelty and contempt of humans. In Britain and America, the mongrel has fought off rabies and distemper outbreaks, high litter fatalities, dog-catchers, mass euthanasia and numerous schemes to wipe him out. Forty thousand were destroyed at one fell swoop by the edict of a lord mayor of London during the plague, and dog-whippers were employed by churches to chuck the homeless back into the streets, using giant forceps clamped on the dogs' skulls. Another scheme was London's annual Dog-Whipping Day, with men and boys setting out at dawn to bludgeon all the dogs they could find, leaving the carcasses strewn in every alley and doorway. A thriving dogskin trade made use of the pelts, and passing mongrels were liable at any time to be knocked on the head and conveyed to the tanner's yard, where nasty things happened to them. Mongrel pets were the chief victims when the dog duty was raised in 1867. Every 1 January when the licence fell due, a new batch stood bleakly in the snow. There have been numerous metropolitan dog-purges, the massacre in Peking in 1984 being the most recent. Victorian Kennel Club judge, Major Harding Cox, devised a 'final solution' for the British mutt and tried to lever it through Parliament. The 'gamin of the gutter' was to be got rid of by means of emasculation, taxation, registration and the wearing of discs to display ownership. Breeding would, in future, be permitted only to pedigree stud dogs; mongrel riff-raff would simply be impounded and destroyed.

Today there are 500,000 strays on Britain's streets, most of them mongrels. Two hundred thousand end up in custody, and at least 30 per cent are put down. The latest 'final solution' has been put forward, sadly, by a doctor. Writing in 1984 in *Community Medicine*, David Baxter of Manchester University called for Britain's strays to be rounded up and slaughtered to reduce pollution of public places and the chance of children catching an extremely rare disease called toxocariasis from putting dog-soiled earth in their mouths. He also considered the cull would reduce the number of dog bites and traffic accidents, which it probably would. The rest of his criticisms fly in the face of a 1976 Government report that exonerated the dog as a source of disease.[5] Dr Baxter claimed, as most dog-cull advocates do, to like dogs, adding to the sum of hypocrisy and cruelty that the mongrel has suffered.

All this, and more, the King of Canids has survived, and not as a scuttling night prowler either, but in broad daylight under our noses, as one of the most efficient and successful of all land animals, unaided, unapplauded and, as far as possible for a domestic species, unsullied by human interference in his choice of mate. The bearer of these genes must be fit or it must perish, and the mongrel's success is a testimony to his hardihood, adaptability and intelligence.

The origins of the mongrel

Some sections of society continue to look down on the True Dog as not quite *bona fido*, as an underdog, an illegitimate, a weed. Here is a vet writing in *Veterinary Practice* in April 1983, saying why he thinks mongrel owners should be forced to have their awful specimens sterilized whether they like it or not:

> I do not maintain that *all* owners of pedigree dogs are conscientious and responsible. What I do say is that having acquired an expensive pedigree, this owner is more likely to develop these qualities than the owner of a true mongrel . . . I would like to quote the case of a mongrel pup brought in for vaccination; we are asked what breed do we think it is? Looking rather dubious I might say, 'Well, I think its mother was a spaniel, but its father must have had a bike.'

As we shall see, the majority of vets are much more worried about inherited diseases and deformities in pedigree dogs than they are about the mongrel's mating cycle, but the same preposterous impression is given by the dictionary definition of the True Dog:

mongrel *n.* an animal, especially a dog, of a mixed breed (usu. in contempt).

The word is supposed to derive from the Old English *gemang*, a 'mingling', or the Old English *mengan*, 'to mix', whereas it might just as easily derive from the dialect word *mong*, meaning a 'crowd'. In any case, such a definition of mongrel is quite wrong, because it assumes that all dogs were once pedigrees like those we have today trotting from show to show, and that these dogs blotted their escutcheons now and then to produce the mongrel population. As there are 150 million mongrels in the world, there are quite a few reasons for doubting this assumption.

The mongrel is not 'a dog of mixed breed'; it is not a dog of breed at all, unless one counts its prehistoric origins or chance crossings with synthetic creatures during the course of its amours, quite contrary to the wishes of 'breeders'. In fact, 'a dog of mixed breed' – that is to say, the progeny of two different 'breed' dogs – is, properly speaking, not a mongrel but a crossbreed. Not that a dog should in any case be despised for cavorting with the coddled, or for sporting suspected beagly legs or a puggy mug. Good luck to him or her. I am not suggesting we should look down on dogs with synthetic bits, or look down on any dog at all. Even pedigrees, God help them, can be splendid, dear creatures, despite any amount of incest, arranged marriages, deformities, forced matings, inherited diseases, commerce, transportation, exhibition and hairbrained human tailoring to conform to curious standards. The stern stuff of which mongrels are made can usually shake off these impediments to health, and the savage mutilation of pedigree ears and tails mercifully cannot be passed on in their genes. No, there's nothing wrong with crossbred dogs, or dogs with a bit of breed in their blood – they are all welcome in what Charles Dickens called 'the great and important family of mongrels'[6] – but the mongrel himself stands head and shoulders above man's mutations as the real McCoy, the King of Canids, the Dog as Nature intended him to be.

The mongrel belongs, not to a breed, but a species, the zoological name for which is *Canis familiaris*. Also included in the species are the many breeds cooked up by man for work or fashion: some 400-odd, and some so odd that they seem to belong to a different species altogether. *Canis familiaris*, the domestic dog, is one of the family Canidae (36 species) of the order Carnivora that evolved some 40 million years ago from a small, shrew-like mammal, Miacis, which also gave rise to the Cats, the Viverrids or mongoosy types, the Mustelidae (weasels, badgers and otters) and the Bears.

The Canids (dog types) evolved as high-heeled hunters with blunt, non-retractable claws and padded feet for tireless running. Elongated jaws, containing 42 teeth for tearing flesh and shearing bone, are so typical of the family that the four 'corner' fangs are called 'canines' in other species as well. A 44 lb (20 kg) mongrel can exert a bite pressure of 363 lb (165 kg).

The Canids pant to cool their blood, have superb hearing and can pick up a scent from 30 yards (27 m) off. Butyric acid found in sweat and carrion, if ingested, enhances the sense of smell, and the Canids not only eat carrion but roll in it. They have glands at the bases of their tails and between their toes for producing chemical traces that mark their faeces and their territory, and their urine contains other traces. The roof of the dog's mouth has two small apertures called Jacobson's organs, with which he 'reads' these deposits. The peculiar grin of the scenting dog, called *Flehmen*, is usually accompanied by a chopping of the jaws as he decodes his information. Dogs had computer technology long before we did!

The Canids are the planet's number one carnivores because, although all these agile, strong, lean-limbed, medium-sized, pelt-bearing hunters eat flesh, they are capable of great versatility of diet and will subsist on lizards, fruit, insects and vegetables and go for days on nothing at all. Canids that form packs (not all of them do) will 'doggedly dog' the steps of prey much larger than themselves and eat it piecemeal as it runs for help.

The wolf-like bears (*Tomarctus*) who founded the Canid family were a North American genus that roamed the plains some 10 or 15 million years ago and had dewclaws in place of the fifth hind toes of their predecessors. Their descendants included the wolves, jackals, coyotes, dholes and the Cape hunting dogs. The domestic dog is believed by most scientists today to have evolved from the wolf. Some specify *Canis lupus pallipes* ('white-footed wolf'), the smaller, southern Asiatic wolf with a variety of pelt colorations. The wolf and the dog share the same chromosome count and the same extraordinary range of expressions and gestures arising from a pack-hunting, social way of life. The dhole and Cape hunting dog also pack-hunt but are less sophisticated: the latter regurgitates his food to relatives as a friendly token, which admittedly many canine mothers do with pups. The dog's bark is thought to have developed from the vocalizations of the wolf, rather than from the singing and yipping of some of the others. The dog may have been encouraged to exercise his vocal chords by the big noise himself, man. Dog owners may be regularly observed talking to their dogs, and my next-door neighbour even says 'Woof woof!' to hers.

There is no evidence that any other wild Canid played a part in the origin of the domestic dog, although hybridization may have occurred later; all Canids can interbreed and produce viable offspring. Nor is there any evidence of a primitive ancestor now extinct, although a few scientists still cling to this conviction and believe the mutt in question may have looked something like the dingo, 'evolved from the wolf–jackal stem prior to man's intervention'.[7] If this were so, of course, then the mongrel would be as uncontaminated by man as the lion or the tiger. Most scientists, though, insist on the wolf as the Dogfather, and one even calls the wolf the 'ultimate mutt'.[8] Those who look down on his descendant the mongrel for scavenging may be interested to know that studies of free-ranging wolves in Isle Royale, on Lake Superior, Abruzzi in Italy and in Germany show him to be a shy, nocturnal part-time scavenger as well, turning over dustbins in his longing for survival.

How could the wolf have been domesticated? Well, primitive man lived cheek by jowl with *Canis lupus*: they hunted the same prey and went to all the same night-spots, and there are many myths and legends linking the two. Man would have killed the wolf, as he has always done, for fun and for fur, if not for food. One day, collaring the cubs raking over the muckheaps or middens, a brainwave may have flashed across Stone Age man's primitive features, which went something like this: 'Well, stone me! If I could rear these, I could use them for hunting! I could tie them up and make a burglar alarm! A sentry, as well as a scenter. And not only that; they would howl back at the night that howls at me, and I wouldn't keep getting all these nightmares. Wife! Come and look at this. I could transport those mammoth tusks on their backs, or on a sled! The draughtwolves could double as draught-stoppers. They could track and search for game on a creeper leash, and if I didn't catch anything, I could kill them and spitroast them. Think what a difference it would make, having something to guard the grain and the livestock instead of trying to get it up that tree! We could even live in a big cave, with grain and goodies on the premises. Their skins, dried, already make warm coats, reversible as camouflage jackets. You could dry the gut to make sewing thread, and even their bladders would make windows. You know what I think, wife? I think this could be the start of a beautiful relationship.' And so it was, and the wolf became a member of man's household to evolve into a major civilizing influence in man's history: the dog.

An isolated breeding colony produces wide genetic variants very quickly, as Russian scientists have discovered with silver foxes in captivity, and the interbreeding of hand-reared wolves would have thrown weird cubs after just a few generations. Curly tails, floppiness and soppiness, short muzzles and anything marking a cub out as friendly or 'different' would have been fostered by the human householders, while aggressive, burly, prick-eared customers were killed or kicked out. By degrees, the interbreeding wolves began to look less like their Dogfather, became more amenable, more dependent, more precocious, prepotent and promiscuous than the wolves elsewhere, and they evolved, according to the prevailing climate and conditions, into various shapes and sizes.

The earliest working canines, the first 'doggie vassals', weren't standardized or divided into 'breeds', but these ex-wolves have been grouped by zoologists into four very general classes, existing around the time of the Bronze Age (*see diagram*). Apart from these four – small, medium, shepherd and haulage – was the rest of the canine population: the independent, the crafty, the adventurous, the wilful, the audacious, the wild, the lazy and the surly – all those who, for one reason or another, were disinclined to demean themselves by serving the Flintstone community, and wanted to be natural dogs. They grew in numbers and made shift for themselves. Those who survived continued to live close to man's encampments, mindful of the possibility of shinbones thrown on the middens and nubile doggie workers peering

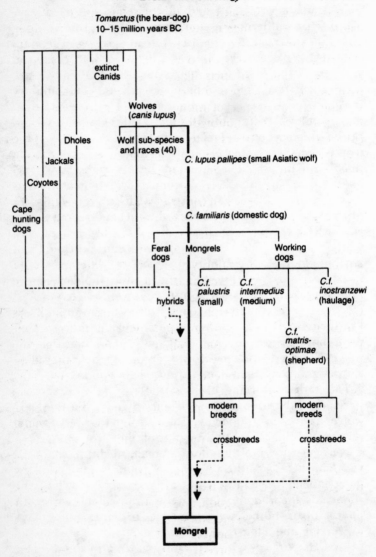

Evolution of the Dog

through the fence, and curious about man, for whom they had a sneaking regard because he seemed to be some sort of pack leader. These freelance mongrels produced hardy offspring and their numbers grew and grew as they mated with wild wolves and, no doubt, the odd wild dog here and there, according to their instincts. They served nature rather than man, and if they displeased her, she extinguished their lines. Among this great race of mongrels, proliferating wherever man lived, were undoubtedly some who were eventually collared for work. Others mated with household stock and lost their pups to man, their genes adapting future generations of slaves and servants. Some mongrels may even, because of their personal charm, have become perfectly useless 'pets' from time to time, casting a spell with a doleful face or a merry wag. But by and large, animals were valued for work or for food, and few mongrels ever heard of a warm bed or a hot dinner.

Now, although the majority of today's 400-odd breeds were developed by man to serve him in some special capacity, most of the early workers were rough-and-ready specimens with no time for primping or prettifying. They were lucky if they fell in the river and got a bath, and any physical beauty they may have possessed was purely accidental. They were judged according to one criterion: could they do the job, or couldn't they? If they couldn't, they rose to independence on the toe of somebody's boot, even if their beauty beggared description. Dogs who did one particular job in one particular area usually came to resemble one another because they would be interbred deliberately to pass on their mental aptitude to their offspring. This is how 'breeds' came about. Linebreeding, and in-breeding (mating father to daughter, brother to sister, etc.), are the breeder's methods of fixing traits. Of course, they fix bad qualities as indelibly as good, and the animals have often to be forced to mate in these incestuous unions, as you may judge by reading pedigree handbooks.

A very early list of breeds in Britain gives the following canine varieties: 'your greyhounde, your mungrell, your mastiffe, your lemier, your spaniell, your hennets, terears, butchers' dogges, bloodhoundes, dunghill-dogges, trindle tails and prick-eared curres'.[9] The mongrel was evidently distinguishable from a dunghill dog (presumably a compliment), but you can see how rudimentary the early classifications were. 'Cur' was used to mean anything from a mongrel to a greyhound,[10] and a Master of Foxhounds recognized only one type of dog: the foxhound. The 'brach', the 'lym' and the 'bobtail tyke' were apparently common; so was the 'spaniell gentle' or 'comforter', said to cure stomach ache. But the modern pedigree dog fad, judging a dog by its looks, is very new. As we shall see, show fever and breed battiness were invented for dogs by mad Englishmen in the 1850s, when dog jobs had largely disappeared and the fighting pits had been prohibited, and suddenly there were a lot of redundant canines about. A competition was devised to take up the slack. Most entries were mongrels in all but name; wild dogs were admitted too. Even fifty years ago, modern 'purebred' dogs generally looked very different from what they do now, as you may see from early photographs or the stuffed exhibits in museums like Tring. Their breeders would have been hard pressed to show you a family tree without mongrels in it, and some went to extraordinary lengths to cover their tracks, inventing 'myths of origin' to account for their 'ancient' breeds. Pride, and no little money, was at stake.

Such ancient *pure* breeds as there were – the Pekinese palace dog, the huge Molossian battle hound of Greece, the baggy bloodhound and skinny saluki – were designed by man for very special jobs and were, so far as nature is concerned, freaks: colossal, shortlived dogs; stunted dogs unable to walk, breathe or whelp normally; spiral-legged dogs; dogs with flaps and folds, barrel chests and bulging eyes, ill-fitting teeth and deformed skulls – none of these would have survived in the wild, but man produced and protected them to do him some service. When their jobs, which had imposed some limits on deformation, eventually disappeared, man let his imagination run riot. Breeding for giant size produces acromegalic features (the jowly look); miniaturization produces pigmy characteristics and achondroplastic features (the stubby look) and breeding for speed produces a dolichocephalic profile (the long-headed look) with extended nasal cooling equipment. These are fairly consistent mutations, and zoologists warn against the common mistake of supposing a direct line of descent between animals of similar appearance in different periods.[11] Don't let anybody intimidate you with tales about his mastiff being directly descended from a Molossian. Chances are, it's a shaggy dog story.

If all this has still not convinced you that the mongrel is the True Dog, and if you still have reservations about the mongrel being 'fit' to stand among pedigree champions, the King of Canids will now deliver his *coup de grâce*: fitness. Here is a list of inherited diseases afflicting pedigree dogs (it is not all-inclusive): overgrowth of gums (gingival hyperplasia), cleft palate, deafness, brachycephalicism (causing a protrusion of the lower jaw and enlargement of the extremities), progressive retinal atrophy, glaucoma, craniomandibular osteopathy (progressive calcification of the jaw muscles), intervertebral disc degeneration, hip dysplasia, tracheal collapse (constriction of the windpipe), luxating patella (slipping knee-cap), cervical spondylopathy (a kink in the spinal cord due to a dorsal tilt), invertebral disc protrusion, elbow displasia, patent molera (braincase gaps), Von Perthès disease, and osteochondritis dissecans, affecting the stifle-joints and hocks of the larger breeds. Dystocia (delivery problems), and respiratory embarrassment, common in breeds with extremely squashed-in faces, may require surgery. And so on and so forth. The Kennel Club, not to say vets, are very worried about this little lot, though the conditions are by no means easy to eradicate.

The following are a few quotes from those in the field of doggie fitness. Nobel-Prizewinning ethologist Konrad Lorenz, himself a breeder:

> It is a sad but undeniable fact that breeding to a strict standard of physical points is incompatible with breeding for mental qualities ... Dog shows in themselves involve certain dangers, since competition between pedigree dogs at shows must automatically lead to an exaggeration of all those points that characterize the breed.[12]

Veterinarian Michael Nelson:

Although most breeders today behave responsibly ... others unfortunately have been intent upon accentuating some particular feature to the detriment of the breed's well-being.[13]

Veterinarian David Coffey:

We now see the physical characteristics of some breeds exaggerated to a point so far removed from the basic canine structure that cruelty is inevitable ... A great deal of time is now wasted by the veterinary profession, not to mention the misery suffered by the afflicted animals, dealing with inherited problems such as hip dysplasia that are the direct result of ill-informed breeding programmes.[14]

Scientist Erik Zimen, who specializes in dogs and wolves:

... These changes are not domestication but real degeneration. It represents a threat to the continued existence of a number of breeds that have a small breeding base.[15]

President of the British Small Animals Veterinary Association (1983–4), Dr Peter Bedford of the Royal Veterinary College:

The mongrel is still a dog, and its hybrid vigour means that the inherited problems of the specific breeds really do not appear. As a pet, I am certain, it is just as revered as its more expensive pedigree compatriot.[16]

Dr Heather Pidduck, of the Department of Genetics, Royal Veterinary College:

From all the work that has been carried out on mice and livestock, hybrid vigour seems to affect fertility, disease resistance, litter size and, to a lesser extent, things like body weight. Strictly speaking, in specialized breeding, where breeders may be creating F-1 crosses (which are the result of a defined cross between pure breeds), hybrid vigour applies progressively less after the first cross; in subsequent crosses it would be halved and halved again. But this would not apply in the case of mongrels, where you get random mating. In this case, the hybrid vigour is maintained because whereas with pedigree animals they are likely to be highly related, with mongrels 99 per cent of the time you're crossing totally unrelated individuals. This means that mongrels should have a higher resistance to canine diseases, although of course, in the case of roaming and feral dogs, they are more exposed to them. But the pet mongrel, properly looked after, has the best of both worlds: it has greater resistance to disease because (a) it's a 'crossbreed', and (b) it is not unduly exposed to infection.[17]

Reason enough, wouldn't you say, to go out and get a mongrel, if you haven't got one already? There are only two drawbacks. One is that, if you acquire a mongrel pup without seeing its parents, you will have no idea what it will look like when it gets bigger – and it may get a lot bigger. The other disadvantage is this: whereas, when a pedigree dies, the unfortunate owner can replace the dog with one very similar, the mongrel, once departed, is not repeatable. There is no consolation for the loss of a friend who, as rude people might say, looked like nothing on earth.

2
Acquiring a mongrel

People who decide that they want a dog, and then acquire a mongrel rather than a pedigree, generally fall into two distinct groups: those who have thought very carefully about it, and those who haven't thought at all.

People who search their hearts and finally choose a mongrel usually do so for the best reasons. They have a settled home where dogs are permitted and which isn't about to be disrupted by a move or a new baby. They can afford the food, the vaccinations and the vet's bills (the People's Dispensary for Sick Animals [PDSA], offering free treatment only to the genuinely hard-up, is *not* an animal NHS). They have thought about the mess, the exercise, the grooming, the carpets, the garden, the fences and the time and trouble involved in looking after a four-legged friend for ten to fifteen years, and they realize that a dog is more demanding than a cat or a tortoise. They have thought about the holidays, and what will happen to the dog when they go away, and they've understood that dogs left alone all day in a house while owners are at work will often show their distress by destruction or barking. The whole family has agreed, including overworked mums and any elderly relatives living at home, that a dog would be welcome, and they have decided where it will be allowed to jump, sit and sleep. And then they have agreed on a mongrel as the best dog to have because they want the animal for itself and not just for what it looks like. They want a friend, rather than a tool, a toy or a status symbol – a True Dog who will follow them like a shadow and stand by them through thick and thin.

The other sort of people who acquire mongrels do so because they are cheap, amuse the children for five minutes and can be easily got rid of when the novelty wears off. In 1987, an estimated half-a-million mongrels scoured the streets, many with their stomachs empty and their eyes popping out of their heads. Hundreds of thousands were dumped on the Royal Society for the Prevention of Cruelty to Animals (RSPCA), Battersea Dogs' Home, the National Canine Defence League (NCDL), rescue societies, sanctuaries, Blue Cross, police and vets. Many more were dropped from bridges, on motorways, in rivers or in dustbins – ex-pets, doormutts, surplus to requirements. In that year 61,615 dogs, the vast majority of them mongrels, were destroyed by the RSPCA and 8169 by Battersea. The animal welfare workers, sickened by the rising tide, plead for changes in the law and save as many as they can: the RSPCA rehomed 53,827 Battersea 9570. Still the animal-loving British public rush out to buy more dogs, new dogs, expensive dogs, and their pets have litter after litter. The shelters, already bursting at the seams, squeeze in a few more, putting two and even three to a cage, until there is simply no more room at the inn. And then the rest are quietly put down, according to one estimate, at the rate of 2000 a day,[1] never to trouble the animal-loving British public again. Before you go out and buy a new dog, please come and look at these secondhand rows. Whether or not you meet a friend, it will bring home to you the enormity of the problem throughout the country, and the callousness with which other people have shrugged off their responsibilities. You will see faces to amuse you, faces to accuse you and, if you have any feelings at all, faces to break your heart. A dog is for life, not just for Christmas.

There are a few questions to ask yourself before you decide on dog-adoption. The first is: Do you really want it? A dog knows no greater anguish than to be abandoned by the owner it loved and this animal has already been through that once. If you think you may be Number Two, please save yourself the trouble. Secondly, I would advise especial caution if you have young children. Any dog, mongrel or pedigree, is capable of biting, and small children playing and experimenting with life will often put a pet under the direst pressure when your back is turned. An adult stray from a shelter may have an angelic temperament but it may have been sadistically abused, or have ingrained bad habits that will take time and patience to alter. It isn't fair on the child or the dog to expect them to hit it off under these circumstances. A young child cannot read a dog's reactions the way grown-ups can; they don't understand where play ends and danger signals begin. There are very few genuinely psychotic dogs who will suddenly bite for no reason at all, but many dogs who have suffered great cruelty in the past will snap if they are frightened or pulled about, at least until their confidence in human beings is restored. After that you can put your head in their mouths or leave them to babysit with equanimity, but do be careful at the outset. Use common sense. The kennel staff generally know which are the problem customers and they will gladly steer you towards a gentle bitch who likes nothing better than kids, kids and yet more kids – as bitches often do. In any case, children must be taught that a dog is not a toy or a squeezebox. Like us, it needs some privacy and respect.

Where to find one

If you want a mongrel, acquiring one is only too easy – they're going begging. The only thing you must not do is to grab one off the streets; a stray of no fixed abode must be taken to the police to be entered in their records. If you want to keep it, the police will ask you to fill in a form and buy a licence, subject to the owner claiming the dog. All other strays are sent by the police to a pound or shelter. In London, Battersea's red vans make regular morning pick-ups from the stations, and an increasing number of local authorities employ wardens.

So far as costs are concerned, the rescue dog *is* a bargain. Not only do most British dogs' homes check the animal's health for you, but they will take back any dog that proves unsuitable. You won't get a fairer deal than that from a pedigree breeder. How much do the shelters charge? It varies, from Battersea's £20–£50 plus £5.00 for vaccination (which includes their pedigree dogs; special rates for OAPs), to nothing at all, although homes that make no charge do ask you to give a donation to the unfortunates left behind, and some officially retain ownership of the dog should anything unforeseen happen to prevent you from looking after it in the future. A few homes run a visiting system, with someone able to give advice and see how your new monster's settling in. Inexperienced dog owners find this a tremendous help, although not all shelters can afford to do it.

Other sources of mongrels are well known. The friend whose bitch has a litter and who asks if you want one of the pups. The friend who asks you to take old Snowy as the owner has been made redundant, the wife's left him and he's off to Saudi Arabia. The advertisement in a local paper: 'Good homes wanted for mongrel pups'. The local vet, who often has unwanted dogs brought in for euthanasia. The local training classes, where somebody's pet is pregnant. These are all good sources because you can see where the animal comes from and can meet a puppy's mother to appraise her size and disposition.

Going down the list, we come to pet shops. Some premises are approved by the Pet Trade Association. Beware of the others; distemper and parvovirus claim many shop-puppies' lives, and there's a heartless trade in tiny, half-weaned babes crated from dealer to dealer across country. In any case, if you *buy* a puppy, you should do so subject to prompt veterinary inspection. If the vendor objects, there is probably something to hide. Never, ever, buy a pup from a market. Their chances of survival are slim, according to a survey,[2] and adult dogs may be stolen.

If you decide on a 'rescue' dog, you are literally saving an animal's life. Many overcrowded shelters are forced to destroy inmates after the statutory seven days, and reports have reached me of some homes putting them down after only four. The dogs locked up on Death Row have committed no crime, and there are many affecting cases of these animals pleading, in their doggie ways, to live. One mongrel about to be put down in Battersea sat up on his haunches and begged with his paws together. He was reprieved by staff, but few are so lucky: nobody wants them.

Diseases and vaccination

People who write dog books are fond of warning readers not to adopt a rescue dog; they say rescued mongrels are dangerous and diseased, and that you should only ever get a puppy from a pedigree breeder. Rubbish. Getting a mutt from a dogs' home has brought as much joy and love to the people I've talked to as spending a king's ransom on a pedigree puppy, and some of the dogs put down for savaging children and adults have had pedigrees a mile long. As to the risk of disease, all the homes I visited gave their dogs a medical check-up before they let them out and vaccinated them against the major diseases. Those with manageable numbers wormed, bathed and de-flead them as well. There is always the chance of infection between animals crowded together, whether it be in a fastidious shelter, a show or a vet's waiting room, and staff at dogs' homes realize the risks and take every possible precaution, watching for signs of incubated disease on their premises. Canine parvovirus broke out, not in these homes, but at pedigree shows and kennels.[3] The new manager of Battersea is himself a veterinary surgeon determined to cut down the risk of infection. Mr Wadman Taylor told me, 'When I was practising in London, I used to say "Don't go near Battersea – it's full of infection." But they didn't vaccinate in those days, and it's made a big difference.'

All mongrels, despite their hardiness, need protection against the killer diseases, the same as pedigree dogs. Survival of the fittest is all very well unless your particular mongrel happens not to be the fittest, and you should be on his side should nature call him to account. Never take an uninoculated dog out and about until its vaccination course is complete: you'd be spoiling the ship for a hap'orth of tar. A puppy is utterly vulnerable and an adult dog transported to a new area runs a terrible risk of local infection. Mongrels are not expensive; the least you can do is to pay for a course of vaccination for the poor little devil.

The major dog killers in the United Kingdom are distemper (and hardpad), infectious canine hepatitis (also known as viral hepatitis and nothing to do with the human version), leptospirosis and canine parvovirus. Distemper, a frequently fatal viral disease, is signalled early on by fever, listlessness and lack of appetite, as well as vomiting. These signs may be followed by coughing, yellow discharge from the nose and eyes, thickening of the skin and footpads, and convulsions. The disease can be transmitted on the air, and even if a dog recovers, he may be left with incurable tremors all his life. A couple of jabs will see your dog or puppy through all these dangerous diseases for the first year, and thereafter one booster per year will usually take care of the lot. Canine hepatitis is a liver disease; leptospirosis has two forms, one of which attacks the kidneys; and canine parvovirus (the name means 'little virus') is a comparatively new form of enteritis that can kill without showing symptoms at all. In North America and Europe, of course, rabies vaccination is required by law, and in the USSR, dog-owners are sent vaccination reminders every year. It really is very important. Pups in kennels and shelters will often, to save expense, be given a 'measles' vaccine against distemper to tide them over. (It was discovered quite recently that vaccination with the measles virus provides at least some protection against the dread distemper.) You should ask about this, and whether you may have a certificate for your vet's reference.

Vaccination will cost you something (the PDSA do *not* offer it free): the standard cost for *all* the major diseases (including parvovirus) is about £25–£35 plus VAT with local price variations, though individual vaccines cost less than that. But you should think of this as part of the purchase price of your pet. A dog without vaccination can be healthy and here today but gone tomorrow, and it will hurt you particularly if it was your fault. Veterinarian Tony Cowie, who often broadcasts on the radio, explains:

> Mongrels are hardier dogs; they have hybrid vigour and I think they can possibly shake off an infection slightly easier, but their actual baseline immunity depends upon what mum had. If she had contact with these diseases, she would pass on a good maternal immunity in her milk to the puppies. This would see them up to the age of about eight to twelve weeks, but then they're just as susceptible as the next guy. If you go to Liverpool or

Manchester, you will see lots of mongrels and lots of pedigree dogs, and lots of endemic distemper, and the mongrels come into the surgery with it just the same as the others.

What about mongrel puppies?

Our vaccination course starts here at eight or nine weeks with another shot at twelve weeks. To be 100 per cent sure, we recommend another at sixteen weeks as there is a percentage of puppies who will not respond fully at twelve weeks to parvovirus inoculation because they may have a high maternal immunity still there.

Please take your new adopted mongrel, pup or adult, to the local vet and he or she will advise you on the type of vaccine for your area, but telephone *beforehand*, explaining where the animal comes from and how old it is. If it's a puppy, it should be carried or taken by car, and if it's too big to carry, the vet will advise you on the phone what to do. In these circumstances, some prefer to make a house call, to save you walking the streets with an uninoculated dog and sitting in their waiting room. (If you don't know of a local vet, you can find a list in the Yellow Pages.)

Choosing one to suit you

You don't have to choose *one* at all: two are just as good, and will often help each other settle in. If they are of opposite sexes, of course, one will need to be neutered, and you should also think in terms of which dog will be 'in charge': animals are not very democratic, and if there is any doubt about their status, they tend to fight. A difference in size or age will help to make up their minds.

The choice of pup or adult, male or female, large or small, smooth or shaggy, will depend entirely on you and your family set-up. What can you handle? The most popular choices are obviously the gorgeous healthy young friendly ones, and these are the easiest to rehome. The more unlovely, scraggy, elderly and miserable a dog looks, the slimmer its chances of impressing anyone. It will probably skulk in the corner, or stare out from its plastic bed, knowing in its doggie mind that its days are numbered. If you don't have children, you might

consider one of these despondent wrecks. They may not like
you at all at first; they may not eat; they may hide behind the
chair. But as you'll see in a later chapter, they can come out like
stars and bluebells, with a little patience.

Pups

Pups, whether you get them from a shelter, shop or friend, are
notoriously cuddly. This is a trick of nature to get you to take
them home, where they will go through a wetting and messing
stage, followed by a teething and tearing stage. Try to look at
the pup as a would-be dog, and you'll get the picture. It may be
intending to grow into something unusual, and today's large-
footed babe is tomorrow's behemoth. Some experts think you
should be careful to appraise a puppy's temperament by its
behaviour in the litter. I don't; I think that you will instinctively
plump for the personality that suits you. You'll feel a little
tug.

Pups have a socializing period between four and fourteen
weeks, and the ideal time to adopt is around seven to nine
weeks. Before that, they need contact with their littermates or
they may grow up unsure of other dogs, and if it's left until
much later, they may have problems adjusting to people.
Hand-rearing tiny orphans is not to be undertaken lightly. If
you're landed with a litter, please talk to a vet, or consult one of
the excellent Popular Dogs books on the subject (*The Popular
Guide to Puppy-Rearing* by Olwen Gwynne-Jones is first class).

A pup should be picked up carefully, using both hands, and
cradled gently. Many dog tots are badly injured by being
dropped, and children are often the droppers. A healthy pup
is wriggly, soft and plump. Its skin is loose and mobile and
flops back into place. There should be no discharge from eyes
or nose: frothy milk down the nose may be a sign of cleft
palate. Coughs or sneezes indicate more than a cold, and pop-
eyes are a bad sign, too. Ears should be clean and not smelly;
teeth should clench perfectly and gums should be pink, not
anaemic-looking. Little thighs should be free of spots and
scabs; black specks in the fur mean flea-dirt, and signs of
diarrhoea mean trouble. Tums should have no lumps or
bumps: umbilical hernias require a minor operation. Limbs

should be strong, rather than rickety. Beware of adopting a cold, skinny pup, unless you are prepared for it to die on you. A bloated appearance, though, simply means worms; you should have the puppy wormed by a vet in any case. Round worms such as *toxocara canis* (about which we have all heard so much) look like pieces of white or pinkish cotton or string, two to six inches (5–15cm) long and coiled like a spring. They may cause coughing, vomiting and diarrhoea in pups, and the eggs, shed in soil, are virtually indestructible. The larval stage can, once in perhaps two million times, cause an obscure, unnotifiable disease called toxocariasis in certain predisposed children if they ingest infected soil. Although the alarmist journalism on this subject has been totally irresponsible, it is best to take precautions. Tell children to wash their hands after playing with pups, make sure your pup (and, later, dog – although only lactating bitches transmit the parasite) defecates away from children's play areas, and have your puppy wormed at four weeks, eight weeks, three months and then six-monthly thereafter. You don't need to fast the little fellow and the medicine is very straightforward, but must be prescribed according to weight. Go to a vet rather than the pet shop; the choice of preparations on the market may lead you to the wrong one.

There is another common parasite found in dogs – the tapeworm, which is flat like a piece of tape and attaches to the dog's bowel by little stickers. Small segments like rice grains or melon seeds break off and wriggle out of the dog's anus all on their own. Tapeworms are usually associated with one of their hosts, the flea, (also with rabbits, rats and other rodents especially in country dogs) so if you see signs of either, ask the vet to prescribe a little something. Tapeworms may cause listlessness and loss of appetite in a pup, but may be symptomless. Parasitic worms, by the way, are common in mammals. Cats have their own, and so do we – threadworms, found in children, are nothing to do with pets.

Adults

Of course, you may not want a pup at all. Mongrels of all ages come in every shape and size, and age can be roughly determined by tooth discoloration, although this may also be due to illness. Yellowish brown stains and bluntness of the canines usually mean the dog is over five years old, unless it smokes a pipe. Dogs go grey like humans, in their case around the muzzle, and older dogs lose their figures too. Please don't write off mutts past their first flush of youth. They still have a lot of mileage in them, are loyal and affectionate and much better suited to retired people than a young tearaway or a puppy. Few get the chance of a home, but with a little judicious dieting, they can live for years.

Mongrels are all bespoke canines – none of this off-the-peg breed nonsense, although crossbreeds do have recognizable bits. If you *know* the dog to be half-labrador, do find out about labs, and similarly with other 'working' breeds. Pedigree traits are fairly predictable and one or two may not be your cup of tea. It's no good adopting a cross-mastiff if you are eighty-five and live in a flat. There are mongrels and crosses to suit everyone's tastes, and if you can't find a soulmate among them, then you're very hard to please.

Ex-dogs' home dogs may need a refresher course in housetraining (*see* Chapter 4). Battersea waifs used to go out with a message on their collars: 'Pray have a little patience with me. There are so many of us shut up together here that the keeper has no opportunity to teach us habits of cleanliness. I am quite willing to learn.' Another difficulty for the adopted dog is a yen to trace its former owner, greatly missed. If you live close to their old haunts, you'll need to keep your adopted one by you, or it will wander off. Give it time; it's a bit confused, that's all. The problem of wanderlust in general is much more common in males than in bitches – though this is not any excuse for letting them roam the streets! Males are assertive and adventurous and need firmer handling, so if you are submissive and shy yourself, you may be better off with a bitch. A dog is rather like a poker player – he will examine you for your aces. Most police dogs are reclaimed rejects and most are males, so you can see what can be done, even with a large, potentially aggressive customer such as the German shepherd, by being firm and kind. However, as one dog section chief told me, 'You don't give a dominant dog to a shy handler, or the dog will be looking to have him over.'

The answer to the question – dog or bitch? – will also depend on which sexual habits you can put up with smilingly. Bitches have an oestrus or season twice a year, each lasting about three weeks. During that time, they lose blood-stained fluid from the vagina and pester you to go out, hoping to be mated. They may, if thwarted, suffer a false pregnancy, start 'nesting' and be snappy if disturbed. They also attract local males who may congregate in your garden. There are drugs and sprays to mask these problems, but they can be prevented once and for all by spaying. Males are not subject to 'heats' – any time is right. If they sense a neighbourhood bitch in season, they become very frisky, wanting to get out. If frustrated, they may make a Great Escape bid, sulk, growl, mark their territory (urine stains a carpet), or make ludicrous attempts to mate with something in the house, such as a cushion or a visitor's leg. Again, such ardour can be controlled by drugs, but the vet may advise castration, and if he does, please listen. Talk of neutering healthy animals may seem cruel, but consider the unwanted mongrel litter your pet may produce if it should escape: life isn't all that grand for them either, and at least your dog has a home. Vets and the RSPCA recommend the neutering of mongrel pets because they see what happens to so many of the puppies. Of course, if you happen to have a gay dog like my own mutt Stanley, the problem doesn't arise. All that concerns him is the whereabouts of another mongrel called Sid.

Appearance and size

Other choices such as coat-type and size are more straightforward. Longhaired luxury requires a lot of work if the coat isn't to become matted, and may cause problems like runny eyes and imbedded grass-seeds. If you don't plan to groom your dog every day, either have it clipped or choose a smoothie. A smooth mongrel may moult in spring and summer more profusely than most, but a Mr Sheen in good condition is softer than mink and smoother than silk. A third type of coat, wiry or woolly, does not moult but needs professional clipping or stripping if you mean to keep it very smart. Wiry and woolly dogs are hardy and have a certain Gaelic charm.

Size? This is really a matter of common sense. The bigger the dog, the more he will cost you to feed and the more mess he will make – of every sort. I know of enormous dogs living happily in flats, but they *must* have somewhere safe to run free outside if they are not to feel cooped up and testy. If you fear burglars, a small dog's bark is just as effective a deterrent as a St Bernard's, and never, in any case, buy a big, boisterous dog for a child. The youngster won't be able to manage and there will be panic, a fight or a traffic accident. Dogs are very strong and even a medium-sized mongrel can drag an adult after a cat. This is where dogs no longer in their prime come into their own – they are more sedate.

You may weigh all these pros and cons, and then go to a shelter and come away with something completely different from what you intended. Don't worry about it. The dog you choose for its very awfulness will, given time, make itself beautiful in your eyes.

Temperament

Appearance isn't everything, as every True Dog-lover knows. What about temperament? For some people, rescuing a stray becomes a pointless exercise unless they can save a lost soul as well – a dog who has been made completely miserable, hostile and scared by somebody else's cruelty. If you are such a person, no praise is too great, and there are enough moving testimonies from those who have succeeded to make it worth a try. But please do it with your eyes open and don't, whatever you do, expect small children to help. Canine salvage is a delicate operation.

There are a few things you should know before you start. Firstly, most of the dogs who have ever savaged anyone have been male. Not all, but most. But any dog who is dominant, unpredictable, surly when reasonably chastised and vengeful by nature is not to be trusted in your home. Secondly, there are very few genuinely mad *mongrels*, since they have not been subjected to close breeding or purpose-breeding for aggression

like certain pedigrees that are known to throw volatile strains.
Most behavioural problems in mongrels are not due to
inherent nuttiness but to bad habits ingrained by mis-
management. Thirdly, if you take on board a mongrel with
these habits, you may be inheriting problems that led to the
previous eviction of the dog, and aggression, dirtiness and
noisiness are the most common. These habits are by no means
impossible to eradicate, but they will take time and patience,
and you must not wallop the dog if he gets it wrong at first.
Forewarned is forearmed.

What do the experts say? Catherine Fisher, respected dog
author and breeder:

> I do not think that any dog is naturally vicious. Aggression – which
> in most cases is a sign of fear – is their only defence against the
> insensate and sadistic cruelty that has been their unhappy lot, and
> though it may take some time, all their fear and suspicion will be
> overcome by kind and humane treatment.[4]

TV vet and author David Taylor:

> My favourite [choice of dog]? The first pup you come across in the
> kennels of the local humane society clinic. That's how I got the
> finest dog one could find – a mongrel bitch pup in need of a home
> before its ten days in Death Row were up.[5]

Vet Dave Grant talking to me about his dog Barny:

> He came into the surgery when he was about eight weeks old – a
> stray with a broken leg. He was treated for shock and taken to the
> RSPCA hospital at Putney where he spent the night kipping in the
> ambulance room because everybody liked him. Then he was
> operated on and sent to a dogs' home, which is the normal
> procedure for strays. I happened to be working down there at the
> time, and one day my wife came down and fell in love with this
> pathetic little specimen coughing his heart out with kennel cough.
> It was Barny again. He was about to be put down. I said, 'Well, we
> can't have that,' so I took him home – where he promptly
> developed parvovirus. We nursed him through that for five days,
> sitting up all night with him, and my wife wouldn't go to Prince
> Charles and Princess Diana's firework display because she was too
> concerned about Barny.
>
> Not many dogs would have lived through kennel cough,
> parvovirus and a broken leg in their first three months, but then
> mongrels have hybrid vigour and Barny's a survivor. I tell him he's
> the luckiest dog in the world; he's an exceptional dog, very very

affectionate and he likes people. He's three-and-a-half now, weighs 35 lb, and he has these enormous ears, one of which he flicks inside out when he's embarrassed.

Tony Blunt, former police dog handler, now in charge of the Hearing Dogs for the Deaf scheme in the UK:

Most of the dogs on our scheme have been mongrels from the rescue centres. People can sell pedigree dogs, but they just turn mongrels out, don't they? They're good intelligent dogs; there's no reason why they shouldn't have a purpose in life just like everybody else. We train them from eight to twenty-four months of age, dogs or bitches, I don't mind either. From taking a dog out of a home for unwanted dogs to the point where you present it as a Hearing Dog to the people in their homes takes about four months.[6]

Author, journalist and mongrel-advocate Jilly Cooper:

As with fostering or adopting disturbed teenage children, you will need endless patience, love and perseverance, but if the rewards are slow in coming, they are even more satisfying in the end. For once again (just as mopping up puddles and coping with the devastation caused by a young puppy cements your love for the little creature), it is the work involved in restoring an adult dog's confidence and gradually winning his love that binds the rescued mongrel and his owner so completely to one another.[7]

Vet Tony Cowie:

Every single one of the five dogs I've had has been a rescue. I've never gone out and bought one. They've been young dogs that people have brought to me and said, 'Put him to sleep.' I say 'No, why not give the dog to me and I'll give it a chance?' I think you've got to assess why the dog is doing what it's doing, and if you go back to basics, there aren't many nutcase dogs that are born nutcase dogs. The majority of dogs end up in rescue, in my opinion, because either they have been acquired for the wrong reasons originally, or they have been treated incorrectly. The majority of dog problems are people problems, and to unscramble them does take persistence and perseverance.

An awful lot of problems with dirtiness and viciousness are caused because there was never enough exercise and discipline in the early stages. A dog growing up is like a child: it needs to be told what 'yes' and 'no' mean. Then there is the sort of problem that the RSPCA see down here a lot, of the genuinely couldn't-care-less owner who maybe got the puppy for Christmas, which by summer has grown into a bigger dog and become a nuisance, and these are delinquent animals – they've had no training at all. But they do train up to be some very nice dogs indeed. Very few dogs are rogues, but you've got to appreciate, I think, that when you get a dog from a shelter, the people who handed it in may not have been totally honest with the staff about its faults – they know there are too many dogs and too few homes and they may have omitted to mention, say, vicious tendencies. So I think with any adopted dog, you've just got to give it a try. Take advice maybe from a veterinary surgeon, from the kennel staff and, of course, from dog-training classes, because you *can* still teach an old dog new tricks.[8]

Manager of the NCDL rescue kennels at Petersfield, Elizabeth Wooltorton:

All I can tell you is, we claim their confidence back straight away. Within forty-eight hours we've got the dogs coming to us, and that's purely because we ignore them while they're in the kennel. They go in, and they've got their little bed made up, and they're fed, and we work round them. We don't go to them. And gradually they realize, 'They're not going to beat me up!' And all of a sudden you've got the nose beside you, and you make a bit of love. Two-thirds of them were climbing the walls when they first came in.[9]

Whether you choose a mongrel adult or a mongrel puppy, and wherever you get it from, life is a lot easier if, at the outset, you put yourself in the dog's place. Ask its previous keepers for details of its diet, and stick to what it's used to at first – this will avoid unduly upsetting a worried tummy. Collect it in the morning if you possibly can; that way it will have time to get used to your house before darkness falls and it has to sleep in a strange bed. Don't make a detour from the kennels to show your new pet to friends; come straight home. For a pup in particular, the journey may be hair-raising. Carry the little creature, don't let it walk in the streets without vaccination, and if you collect it by car, take an old towel because it may be sick. Have someone with you if you can, to comfort the dog as you go along. Have everything ready at home *before* you arrive: its water and food bowls, its bed or box, and lots of newspaper for toilet training. Have the garden fixed up: it's no good mending the fences once the Bitzer has bolted. Protect your prize bulbs – don't wait for the newcomer to dig them up and then give it a hiding. And finally, please, please don't bring your mongrel home for a Christmas present. Noisy festive seasons are not the time to be housetraining a frightened orphan. Remember: 'A dog is for life, not just for Christmas.'

3

Visiting the shelters*

What would Britain do without its charitable dogs' homes and shelters? Government contingency plans for dealing with the next rabies outbreak in the United Kingdom show how much we take for granted our network of waif-collecting centres and the dedication of a small band of animal-lovers fighting to make ends meet without official help or government aid. The British public may like to think that, when they abandon their pet dogs by the hundred thousand, they go directly to some sanctuary in the sky where they get free Bonio biscuits and everything is quietly taken care of. The truth is very different. Here on earth behind the shelter walls, dogs stand in barrack blocks, waiting and hoping, flattening their noses against the bars when they hear human footsteps. And the kennel staff who love them and cannot find them homes get the dirty job of walking the dogs as jauntily as they can to their electrocution or their overdose of barbiturates, while somewhere far away sit their blithely oblivious ex-owners.

Everywhere, little sanctuaries struggle to survive. From the St Francis Charity for Stray Animals in Dorset, manager Eileen Roberts writes:

> My sister and I, with a small number of friends, have been rescuing dogs and cats, horses and rabbits for a number of years, and have actually carried out the rescues ourselves. We have suffered a lot of hardship and abuse. Although we are now a small registered charity, we have always worked, and still do, for funds to feed these animals . . .

* For addresses and telephone numbers of homes and shelters, see Appendices.

Daphne Whailing of Animal Concern in Warrington, Cheshire describes a similar situation:

> Every city and town has its animal problem to a greater or lesser degree, and there are few if any homes to come anywhere near to Battersea. On the contrary: most homes are too sad and depressing for anyone to visit . . . I decided to throw in my lot with the Warrington branch of the RSPCA, for here one man had taken it upon himself to set up a desperately needed animals' home for the area. But five years on, after oh so many let-downs and disappointments, his dream is three-quarters finished. It has been a hand-to-mouth struggle.[1]

Animal welfare work in Britain may draw on a huge reservoir of popular sentimentality, but when you turn on the tap, a mere trickle comes out. Only a handful of the sympathetic people actually *do* anything to help the dedicated few, yet somewhere among the homes and shelters there may be a future friend of yours, pushing his or her snout through the wire netting, thinking perhaps tomorrow you may come. So I went along to some of the country's sanctuaries, window-shopping on your behalf, as it were, and meeting the rough diamonds on display. A bit depressing? Not if you intend to take one home. It was like being at large in a jewellers' silly sale.

The Dogs' Home, Battersea

Battersea is not a bad place at all: in fact, one morning the staff found Blackie, a fat black mongrel, sitting outside the front gate on his own, waiting to get in. He'd been rehomed to five different places but kept getting evicted or brought back in for chasing bitches, so he'd decided to save his sixth or seventh owner the trouble and return of his own accord. The food wasn't bad here, and they have underfloor heating and infra-red health lamps, plus lots of bitches in cages that you could leap over if you took a run-up. The staff felt so sorry for Blackie after all his rehomings that they clubbed together and took him on a day trip to the seaside. He now sits, neutered, aged and portly, in reception, lord of all he surveys.

There are other permanent residents, like Tina, a lovable black-and-tan bitch who came in pregnant and snappy; Tramp, the would-be German shepherd who arrived as a bag of bones; and Leila, the cross-collie who refused housetraining and showed herself up destroying shoes. She was brought into the surgery with a torn mouth, and now sits there all the time, watching consultations. Once she was sold, jumped out of the car window in Battersea Park Road and raced back again. Leila likes it in surgery.

Since 1860, when it was founded by Mary Tealby, Battersea has taken in over 2½ million strays. In 1986 it received 15,720 mongrels of which 7274 were sold, 1875 reclaimed and 6571 went begging. Battersea dogs cost between £20 and £50 'according to breed and condition', says the information leaflet. Manager and veterinary surgeon Mr Wadman Taylor explains, 'If we get good pure-bred dogs, we usually place them through the Breed Rescue.' The rest are all effectively 'mongrels', some resembling pedigrees and some not: 'Healthwise, they are just as good to have.' Prospective owners pay 50p (20p for OAPs) to walk round the serried ranks, raising and dashing doggie hopes and assailed by dog swearwords as they walk away.

Charles Dickens visited the home in 1862 when it was a dying dogs' asylum in London's Hollinworth Street, the butt of complaints and jokes in *The Times* ('Why not a home of refuge for all the starving butterflies and caterpillars of the gardens of London?'). What struck Dickens particularly was the contrast between the frantic inmates here, simply dying to catch his eye, and the well-fed contestants at the nearby Islington Show, the forerunner of Crufts, who wouldn't have wetted on him if he'd been on fire: 'At Islington there were dogs estimated by their owners at hundreds of pounds. Here there are animals that are only, from a humane point of view, worth the drop of prussic acid which puts them out of their misery.' Most affecting to Dickens, with his strong sense of outrage on behalf of the unwanted and the underdog, was the sight of the mongrels.

> Poor beast, with his tail left, not to please Sir Edwin Landseer, but because nobody thought it worth while to cut it, with his notched

pendant ears, with his heavy paws, his ignoble countenance and servile smile of conciliation, snuffling hither and thither, running to and fro, undecided, uncared for, not wanted, timid, supplicatory – there he was, the embodiment of everything that is pitiful, the same poor pattering wretch who follows you along the deserted streets at night, and whose eyes haunt you as you lie in bed after you have locked him out of your house . . . I think it is somewhat hard that [people] should turn the whole scheme into ridicule.[2]

How many inmates are there now, I asked Mr Wadman Taylor? 'Today we've got over 700 and only 475 kennels, so at this time of year we're always doubling up and trebling up in some cases' (there are peaks at holiday times and after Christmas). What does the prospective purchaser have to do? 'We ask them all the relevant questions, because we've got to sort out whether they're genuine people or whether they want a guard or performing dog or whatever – we only sell them for pets. We ask the applicants if they have had a dog before, and what sort they had; we ask if their children are used to living with a dog, whether they have a cat, whether they have room for a dog and time to look after it, and so on.'

What are people generally looking for – one that will live long and prosper? 'Most people don't do it logically like that. They take the one that attracts them for some non-specific reason!' All the dogs that go out have been given a 'medical', and if they have fleas, for example, or mange, 'we'd treat them before we let them out. Of course we can't isolate for infection with over 700 dogs in 475 kennels, but we do vaccinate, and people can bring a dog back here within seven days for any reason and get their money back, or if they think it's unwell, we'll treat it for them free of charge.'

Temperament? 'Occasionally we get gifts to the home that are very nice dogs and we know quite a lot about them, but if it's a stray that hasn't been with us long, obviously we know nothing of its character. Some dogs don't take to being kennelled, so with some that don't appear to have good temperaments, it's simply that they've been institutionalized, and when they get to the right sort of home they can be restored to perfectly normal pets. There are noisy barkers, for example, but most can be rehabilitated to some extent.' To try to ensure that the owners and their new dogs are well suited, in 1983 Battersea appointed two visitors as part of a much-needed after-care service. Most puppies now go to Battersea's new kennels at Bell Mead, their country annex at Old Windsor. Retired people may, in any case, consider a 'golden oldie': 'It's better for elderly people than having a young puppy.'

The unwanted and ailing dogs are destroyed, but gone are the days of prussic acid, and the lethal cage on wheels for dispatching fifty dogs at one time with carbonic acid gas and chloroform. Gone, too, is the electrothanator still used by some other welfare organizations. 'I came here at the end of April '84, and in June we began using intravenous barbiturates instead. I know which way I'd prefer to go, given the choice: it would certainly be the anaesthetic. The Committee wanted to do away with the electric cabinet for a long time but couldn't do so until they had a resident veterinary surgeon, and I have three qualified veterinary nurses here as well.' How long do the dogs have before it comes to that? 'Well, they've got to have seven days by law, but they all have longer than that unless they're very ill or better off in the next world. Usually they hang on for several weeks, in the hope that somebody will take a fancy to them.'

The National Canine Defence League (NCDL)

'A Dog is for Life, not just for Christmas' is the slogan of the National Canine Defence League, founded in 1891 at Crufts Dog Show by Lady Gertrude Stocks. Today the League has fourteen branches, each housing 70–120 dogs, and all of them always full. The kennel staff are very protective of their charges: they mind them and they mend them, restoring broken dogs that have been dragged behind cars and shivering bonebags that have been thrown away in the street. No healthy dog is ever destroyed. The staff rehabilitate them and give them to people who promise to treat them as kindly as they do themselves.

Anyone wishing to adopt a League Dog (for so they remain all their lives for their protection) telephones and makes an interview appointment. The kennel managers invite you and your family to come along and complete a questionnaire to determine what sort of dog you're after – what size, type, age and so forth – and what you could reasonably cope with in your home (not kennelled outside or chained up, please). Once they have satisfied themselves as to your sincere intentions, they will introduce you to suitable canine candidates, and if you find one you like, you simply fill in an adoption form. The NCDL asks for a donation to the dogs left behind, but there's no charge for the dog you adopt and all the kennels make a loss. If you are kind enough to join the League (£7.50 subscription, OAPs £3.45) they are only too pleased, and you get free public liability insurance up to £1 million on damage caused by your dog, a free identity disc engraved with your name and address and free advice on dog ownership to see you through any teething troubles – new homes are visited whenever possible.

At Petersfield, Hampshire, which is the branch I visited, an impressive array of characters peer from the admittance block, the general blocks, the newly modernized hospital, and the sponsored block, where the no-hopers live out their days pleasantly listening to Radio 2 and sleeping in League fleece-lined plastic beds. There was Duchess, the office mongrel, found pregnant in a drainage ditch; Churchill, a bouncy dog named after another bouncy dog called Winston; Hoppy, the basset-cross who howls and howls; Millie, the charmer with the cheesecake grin; Poo, the white poodle who came in black; Godfrey, the naughty lurcher; lots of poor greyhound failures from the flapper tracks, and lots and lots of delightful mongrels with faces as individual as people's.

'I should think 70 per cent are mongrels', says PR officer, Clarissa Baldwin. 'Pedigrees usually go to the Breed Rescue because it does leave room for another mongrel here. The NCDL provide all the mongrels for the Hearing Dogs for the Deaf scheme in this country, beginning with Favour two years ago.' A face peered from Kennel 6 with particular interest. This was Tramp, a glorious grey mongrel who had been a divorce victim. 'He came on *Sixty Minutes* with me when I was interviewed about dogs from broken homes,' said Mrs Baldwin, 'and he was *so* good on television, we expected the calls to come flooding in. Nobody rang about him. Nobody wanted him.'

Many inmates have been thrown out at the peak eviction-age of around six months, doggie delinquents with no training whatsoever but leaping with enthusiasm – 'Young idiots', as manager Elizabeth Wooltorton put it, 'who've been allowed to run riot.' The League spay all bitches old enough to have a season and castrate males on veterinary advice, 'for aggression, wandering and leaping over the fence. It makes them home bodies. We've never had any failures; if we have a dog returned, we usually have to have it castrated because we've got to do something to rehome the dog again and it does help, although it takes six months for the hormones to change. There really is nothing else apart from retraining, and we can only do so much here in a kennel environment. They need to go to someone in a real home who's willing to give them time. They're social people, dogs; they need the time.'

If you want to take on a problem dog, the League like you to have had some experience, and no little dog-squeezing children for fear they would be bitten. 'We never show anybody anything that is unhealthy by *any* means (the dogs are all inoculated and bathed), and of the majority of them up there, there are only two or three that I would have any reservations about, and even they could possibly go to homes that haven't got children. Children are a pain so far as difficult dogs are concerned. The dogs have got to have time spent on them, and go to training classes. You've got to have dominance, without beating the dog up. Start as you mean to go on, because once they've got dominance over you, you've lost. We can't let them overpower us here or we'd have terrible trouble. In the six years I've been here, I think we've had five, maximum, that we've been unable to cope with. About half of one per cent, if that. Within forty-eight hours, these dogs will come to us – and once you've got a nice dog with its confidence back and it loves you, you've got a devoted friend for life.'

The Wood Green Animal Shelters

The Wood Green Animal Shelter at King's Bush Farm, Godmanchester in Cambridgeshire, is the prototype 'space age dogs' home'. It has computer technology and revolutionary parasol-plan kennels, advanced isolation and sterilization facilities and all mod cons. In fact, it's a sort of Ideal Home for dogs. 'These are a completely new concept of kennel', explained Chief Executive Graham Fuller, showing me the parasols. 'The idea is to get away from the barrack block concept. In the centre of each parasol we have the nice cosy sleeping and feeding area where you don't want bright light or a lot of disturbance, and raised sleeping areas are out of the draught. The ventilation in here consists of a reversible fan to either exhaust foul air in the conventional manner, or to use the centre of the parasol as a manifold, so exhausting foul air through individual segments of the parasol (therefore dissipating the air in the minimum time to the atmosphere rather than condensing it and exhausting through a common cowl). The fans automatically increase air change on temperature rise. The kennel staff can come in and see all the kennels at a glance. But outside this controlled central environment – so well insulated it isn't true – the parasol "fans out" into runs with an outlook over a fair spectrum of land and the dogs can look out upon fields, people, animals and activity: they can see practically everything that a normal domesticated dog would see. We've even got piped music in here, because you want to recreate the sort of sounds and smells that the dog is going to find in a domestic environment.' It keeps the dogs normal, instead of turning them into asylum cases.

There are isolation parasols and stringent hygiene procedures in line with a modern human hospital. When rabies comes, King's Bush will be ready for it. All new admissions receive a veterinary examination and are vaccinated and wormed before they go into their designated parasol and shower system. Very plush! Covering thirty acres, King's Bush is one of the largest animal shelters in the country, running, according to Mr Fuller, at half the unit cost per-animal-housed that another leading animal charity has recently spent.

It would be difficult to fault the Wood Green Animal Shelters for either organization or care. At the more olde worlde Heydon Shelter, the dogs and cats live in their own little villages rather than kennel blocks, running as freely as possible. They even have a fountain in their garden – 'It helps to keep down the vermin in the summer and besides, the dogs like it.' Grot, a wildly scruffy Jack Russell, rushes up and down outside the long wire-netting fence barking abuse at a miscellany of lodgers including shaggy and shiny mongrels and an Alsatian in a plaster cast, whose leg had been paralysed due to a road accident. Some of these dogs, like the goats and ponies in the paddock, have been hideously treated.

'One little dog particularly comes to mind,' says Mr Fuller, 'who was terribly terribly burned, not just once but systematically over a long period. She had old scars, and all down one side there was no pelt at all. Yet she was the kindest, nicest little dog you could wish to have, and she went to a home where she is now as happy as a sandboy. There was never any aggression from her at all. But then you get the other side of things, when a dog has been beaten and teased – teasing particularly makes problems of aggression harder to overcome – and with these dogs it's a question of confidence and building a relationship. We find that, with aggressive dogs, unless they have been *trained* to be aggressive, the best way to get over it is just to keep them with you. Never let them out of your sight or smell. We find with Alsatians we've rehabilitated -- these two gentle ones here once bit everything in sight – that it works better if we keep them in the house. We take them to bed, even to the lavatory, and they come round very quickly regaining their confidence. Of course, when one gets down to the sad practicalities of this world, it *is* a case of time and effort, and you have to consider where it is best spent.'

After years of experience – and since they developed their computer system that's about 21,000 dogs, 16,000 cats and 3000 other animals on record – Wood Green staff believe that most aggression-related problems are not inherited; they are environmental. Grot's brother, for example, was destroyed by a vet seven or eight months after he went out because of constant biting and snapping. Grot, now lying on the Fullers' sofa with his feet up in the air dreaming of the mightiest-ever rump steak in the world, is as friendly a scruffbag as you could meet. 'This is why we tend to keep animals differently from the majority of organizations.' Roughly 12 per cent of incoming dogs are strays off the streets; the rest are from previous owners. Wood Green operate a home-to-home policy, encouraging people to bring unwanted dogs in '*before* they get to the stray stage'. That way they remain normal and home-loving, and the staff can build up a dossier on the animal's care and character to help its new 'keepers' (as adopters are called). 'We don't want the animal to come back; we want it to go to a stable environment. We retain control of the animal, issuing an engraved identity disc, and our conditions of adoption are a form of bailment.'

Wood Green has the best possible after-care service and visiting system and there is the inevitable form-filling in reception to ensure that you are the 'kind and responsible' sort of owner. The staff encourage you to come along with your whole family and the pets you may already have, and take your Intended for a walk to see how you all get along. They ask you to see that your new pet is neutered and re-vaccinated, and they hope you will all live happily ever after. Dozens of rehomed mongrels wag from photographs on the walls, sent in by proud 'keepers' who consider Wood Green dogs, rather like Brodie girls, to be *la crème de la crème*. Wood Green also now run a National Pet Register. A lifetime registration fee of £3.00 gets you an identity disc for your dog and his details go on the database computer, to trace him if he should ever go missing.

Royal Society for the Prevention of Cruelty to Animals (RSPCA)

The RSPCA have received a lot of unlooked-for publicity recently because they put down large numbers of healthy animals for which homes could not be found. Since 1824, the society has been a receiving house for the nation's discarded pets, yet all that seems to concern its critics are the niceties of how the undesirables are disposed of – the Huelec electric cabinet, which the RSPCA believe to be the most humane method, has come under special attack. To set the record straight, in 1980 the society rehomed 48,008 dogs; in 1981, 47,871; in 1982, 51,457; and in 1987 they found homes for an amazing 53,827. This means that, since 1980, without the RSPCA, 201,163 *more* unwanted dogs would have starved, died in accidents or been destroyed by vets and charities elsewhere. Perhaps the critics would like to do the dirty work themselves, or else suggest how more homes can be found.

The society has an inspectorate of 270, and 137 shelters, centres and clinics in England and Wales. These include fifty-nine homes where dogs can be adopted, and where their temperaments are assessed for suitability as pets. The society has thrown its full weight behind the national neutering campaign. Headquarters issue publicity leaflets: 'BRITAIN'S DOMESTIC ANIMAL POPULATION IS OUT OF CONTROL. Every year the number of unwanted and abandoned pets increases. The neutering of all pet dogs and cats has the wholehearted approval of the RSPCA. It is *not* beneficial for a bitch to have "just one litter", a neutered animal does *not* undergo a personality change and become fat and lazy, nor does the operation have any detrimental physical effects.' You can visit your local RSPCA clinic for expert advice on the subject and they will also explain about pet health insurance, which they warmly recommend to save you money on vets' bills (excluding neutering and vaccination).

I visited the RSPCA's Patcham Animal Sanctuary at Brighton, founded in 1962 by the Mid-Sussex and Brighton branch, where boarders help pay for the homeless and the dogs receive temporary vaccination and a medical check-up. A tri-coloured mongrel bitch strove to squeeze through the bars to give me a kiss, a greyhound full of sorrow stared out from his plastic bed, and umpteen archetypal black mutlies with floppy ears leapt and cavorted, hoping to pass themselves off as little pups. There was a fearful racket of barking in protest at my not taking everybody home. 'We have about thirty in now,' said Treasurer and dog's-body Philip Hale. 'The turnover in a year is probably 700–800 or more. It has got worse over the last twelve months, but because people round here see the cases of bloody cruelty we get publicized, they come in and give a dog a home. We don't sell them. We ask for a donation of at least £15 to help meet our running costs. That way the dogs remain our property, and if they are ill-treated, in theory at least we can go and take them back.'

Patcham has a scrupulous pre-visiting and after-care system to cut down the number of mismatched dogs and owners who would otherwise be bringing the animals back in again, dissatisfied. 'Some people don't seem to realize that the dog has to settle down and adjust to its new surroundings. They think you should hand them a perfect dog. So we go and visit the prospective owners' home beforehand and made sure that they know what they're taking on. That way everybody's happy.'

A furious barking follows me around the kennels. Was this not aggression? 'A lot of dogs seem aggressive in kennels; you find that everywhere. When you get these out, they're as placid as me,' said Mr Hale placidly. He has himself bent over backwards and sideways to save individual dogs from what he calls 'the chop'. At home he has a shiny mongrel bitch with big ears called Adi, very soft and affectionate, who puts her face in your lap trustingly. Philip rescued her himself and rehomed her twice, only to find she had been rejected for 'dirtiness' and 'running away'. He finally saved her from imminent destruction by palming her off on a long-suffering girlfriend, who now dotes on poor Adi and says she is clean and good as gold.

Dogs still seem to trust us, despite being burned, bludgeoned, hanged and stabbed. In 1987 the RSPCA investigated 85,419 complaints of cruelty, administered 6,259 'verbal cautions' and sent 125 written admonitions from HQ obtaining 1805 convictions and 26 prison sentences and 13 suspended sentences. Not much of a haul, is it, for so much cruelty? The law, however, is not on the animals' side, and only the most monstrous viciousness gets brought to book. 'Dogs suffer more than any other creatures at the hands of men, women and children who invent every imaginable – and unimaginable – abuse and cruelty to inflict on their helpless victims,' says the society. 'Crimes against animals that are punishable by law are more common, more varied and more sophisticated today than ever before.' Reading some of the case histories, I must confess, made me want to go out and commit the odd murder myself. I asked Philip Hale how it could be that dogs don't hate us. 'They have an inherent love of mankind, for what it's worth. I don't think he'll ever knock it out of them.'

St Francis Charity for Stray Animals

Sisters Audrey and Eileen Roberts have given a home to about 120 animals over many years, including dogs, cats, horses, donkeys, goats 'and some sheep once'. It's a small concern: 'We raise money by holding a mini-market every Thursday all the year round in Shaftesbury British Legion Hall main carpark. Thursday happens to be my sister's day off,' Audrey explains.

They are always short of funds, and always rescuing mongrels from a fate worse than death. There was Rusty, for instance: 'We had him from Bath dogs' home. He was a dear little man who had been left to wander on the moors near Bath. Why he had been kicked out, I will never understand. He was so quiet at the home, as though he had given up hope, and all the way to our house he kept staring up at us to make sure it was true and he now belonged to someone.' Tess, 'a darling of a bitch, had all her legs broken as a pup from being thrown down a mineshaft in Wales. Luckily she landed on a ledge about forty feet down, or she would have died. We think she survived by drinking drops of water off the wall until a young miner got her up.' Dusty, a little black chap with enormous ears, was adopted as a pup: 'He was seen being thrown out of a big car with children in it, which slowed down to toss Dusty into a carpark and then quickly picked up speed again. At the moment we have mongrels Titch and Noddy, Nicky the poodle and a Jack Russell, Butch. The landlord of our tiny rented cottage does not want more than four dogs here at a time; we use local boarding kennels for the other dogs taken in, and for about sixty cats and kittens. We have spent hours in bitter winds catching strays and our dream is to have a house of our own with some ground where we can work at rescue on a bigger scale. Our fund-raising mini-market is held every Thursday, winter and summer, from 9 a.m. to 5 p.m.'

Well worth a visit, if you're in the vicinity, as indeed are all the shelters mentioned. You may find the dog of your dreams.

4
How to have a homebody

Before we get down to the nitty-gritty of homebody training, a few general words of advice. If you do not train your dog, your dog will train you. Mongrels are in a very high league mentally and they are great survivors. This means they are in a good position to do as they think fit, if you allow them to. They have strong views on doggie government and how they wish to conduct their affairs – a mentality born of hardship and generations of having to fend for themselves. So if you bring a mongrel home, be it an adult or a puppy, you should expect to spend some time showing it the house rules, otherwise you may end up with a dog despot who grudgingly lets you sit on one of his chairs only when it's quite convenient. A tiny pup's funny little way of gnawing the table legs and leaping at grandad's trousers may be magnified in six months' time to large and very unfunny proportions, and if you adopt an adult dog, you will need to set the tone of your relationship from the very start. If you do not assume authority, you will leave a vacuum that your mongrel will quickly fill, particularly a male dog, accustomed to competing for all his wants.

The traditional theory of dog training or 'breaking' (note the expression) has always been based on dominance: the concept that you impose yourself on the dog as his new pack leader, to be feared and obeyed. Whether or not you subscribe to this draconian view, and an increasing number of trainers and scientists question it, the 'show it 'oo's boss' philosophy has undoubtedly given rise to a great deal of cruelty, sticks, switches, electric shock collars, spiked chains and choke chains to physically coerce the dog into obedience. It is perfectly possible to have authority over a dog without physical cruelty, and if you are dealing with an adult animal from a shelter, you have a particular responsibility to avoid brutal coercion, not only on ethical grounds but because brutal methods may force the dog into a corner from which its only recourse is savage revenge. Wolves, which sort out their internal status feuds on the 'alpha dominance' principle (being led by a dominant 'alpha' male and female), may be closely related to dogs and awfully wild and grand, but they also have horrific and fatal fights.[1] If this is the basis on which you wish to train your dog, one or both of you may end up very badly injured. Dogs have forty-two teeth, humans thirty-two. A big dog can exert a bite pressure of over 600 lb. It's up to you.

The other way of training a dog is to act as senior partner, based on the principle that you *know* more than he does. This method is pretty straightforwardly based on three rules: be firm, be fair and be kind. Put yourself in the dog's place and try to simplify things for him (or her – I use the masculine only as a convention). Remember, he's just a dog. He's not as clever as you. He may be more in tune with nature, more able with his nose and ears, and more faithful than humans can comprehend, but don't expect him to understand cause and effect the way you do, or the whys and wherefores of his behaviour. An obvious point, you might think, but then you'd be surprised how many dog-owners believe this of their dogs and talk to them as though they were members of Mensa.

You may have to go over something again and again with your dog before he sees what you have in mind. Be consistent, and be patient. A dog's greatest happiness is to be 'best pals' with his owner and he desperately wants to live with you and not be turned out and abandoned, so *praise* is the North-West Passage into his thinking. Praise is always remembered better than admonition because the latter is painful to recall, so try to engineer a dog into a position where you can praise him for something if you can, rather than moaning at him all the time. Never, ever, lose your temper with him. Count to ten and start again.

The easiest way is to return to basics. For example, if you

bring home an adult dog with some ingrained bad habit, try to work out the reason for his behaviour: what he fears and what he gains by it. Use your insight. A dog is an animal, incapable of understanding human morals, and only learns what he can and cannot do by his owner's responses. These can be very puzzling, and a dog can make the wrong associations through inconsistency and confusion. He may have been inadvertently 'rewarded' in some way for doing what he really should not be doing, and he may have drawn the wrong conclusions about what is required of him. Bad habits are not always sheer naughtiness; there is often bad teaching behind them somewhere. A dog cannot grasp the concept of 'guilt' or 'evil' (whatever interpretation you put on its facial expressions), or threats of future reprisals, or wrongdoings of yesterday being punished today, or complex verbiage upon the theme of good behaviour. Simplify, and you will see the situation from the dog's viewpoint. Then the remedy will present itself because, with your superior brainbox, you can think one step ahead.

Assuming authority

Some people have natural authority over a dog. Something in their tone of voice tells the animal: 'This is a person to be obeyed.' (Dogs are great admirers of charisma.) If you don't have this natural authority, you will have to assume it, and this will not be achieved by ranting and raving, or waving your arms in the air like a Ferrari mechanic. Crises will inevitably occur in your relationship with your dog: it happens to everyone. Don't panic. You are still in control because your brain is the equivalent of an enormous computer and it will come to your aid in a minute! Drop your voice an octave. Squeaking shows lack of control. Be determined, slow down and be prepared to repeat yourself. Keep your head still – this denotes authority – and keep your back straight and your arms at your sides so that you present a solid shape rather like a lighthouse. In a quiet moment about the house, practise throwing your voice at the far wall like an actor. Laurence

Olivier (now Lord Olivier) once observed that an audience respects the power of an actor who never has to fully extend himself. Dogs are like audiences; they know by your delivery if you're straining.

Try to avoid head-to-head confrontations, big 'scenes' and battles of will. A dog can be easily diverted from a bad pattern of behaviour at the onset by simple planned tactics. One of the best diversion stratagems I've seen was demonstrated to me by the country's leading authority on 'problem' dogs, animal behaviour consultant Dr Roger Mugford. This involves the use of an old coat or towel thrown on the floor, a rape alarm and a few nourishing titbits. At the outset of a dotty turn, the rape alarm is set off, the dog is led briskly on the lead to sit on the coat or towel, and a titbit is given, followed by much praise. I've seen the method employed in Dr Mugford's surgery to great effect on biters, barkers and delinquents. A few such exercises can reform even the most entrenched bad habits by substituting a new pattern of behaviour.

Another very useful tip on the initial homecoming of a known 'problem' dog comes from kennel managers at the shelters, who say the best way to rehabilitate the beastie is to keep it with you constantly, never letting it out of your sight or scent but at the same time ignoring it and going about your business quite normally. Let the dog see your routines and that you do not intend to harm or smother him, and he will come to you when he is ready. Only a tiny percentage of problem dogs fail to respond when they find themselves safe and sound.

What you will need

Many, many mongrel owners simply cannot be bothered about their dogs. Yours is lucky. It has you. Your dog will never join (or *re*join) the tragic, vagabond community roaming the streets, left to foul footpaths, worry livestock and cause thousands of traffic accidents every year. Your mongrel will be a homebody, with a collar and lead, proper walks and a little bed to go to when life gets on top of him, rather than a marauding stray, living in the shadow of destruction.

Leads, collars and halters

A collar and lead are your dog's first steps to civilization. A rolled leather collar, or a flat collar with a metal nameplate that can be engraved with your address and telephone number, are ideal. If there's no nameplate, you can attach an identity disc by the key-ring principle, though these sometimes get lost. The collar and identification are required by law when your dog goes out. The lead should be of strong bridle leather or nylon, 3½–4½ ft (1.06–1.36 m) long (depending on *your* height), with a bolt-action trigger hook to attach to the collar. (The dog's size is not the determining factor because the lead should be slack as you walk.)

Collars are too tight if you can't get two fingers under them when they're done up, and too loose if the dog can jerk its head out and get away. For a very small adult without much pulling power, a harness may be better. Some little dogs suffer from windpipe problems that can be aggravated by a collar.

You may also consider some training equipment to make your life easier. A Flexi-lead, which works rather like an angler's winch, unreeling and locking, or a training lead of nylon cord, 30–45 ft (9.15–13.70 m) long with a hook collar clasp at the end, can be bought at most decent pet shops and will give you control over your dog even at a distance while he's learning the ropes. You can even attach a hook clasp to a washing line if you have one to spare! A little pup will need an interim 'baby' collar and lead; don't spend a lot on this as it will be quickly outgrown.

Many trainers recommend the choke chain, which they call, euphemistically, a 'check chain'. It works by chain-choking the dog when it pulls and, worn the wrong way round, can be catastrophic. Injudicious use of choke chains has caused serious injuries, neuromuscular disorders from constriction of the cervical region of the spine, ruptured windpipe, bruising to the outer and inner ear and epileptic fits triggered by constriction of blood supply to the brain. Animal behaviourist Dr Mugford has invented an alternative to the

choke chain, the 'Halti' (*see illustration*). Dr Mugford says, 'The best place to put your choker is in the wastepaper basket.' He told me, 'The Halti is part of my little battle against animal abuse. It seems a contradiction in a civilized society that we should strangle our friends with bits of metal, but then you get the problem of the little old lady who can't control her labrador without a choke chain. So we went back to first principles. How does a man control an enormous, powerful animal like the horse? Not with a chain round its neck, but by moving its head around. So the Halti is based on the equine halter.'[2]

Insurance

Veterinary treatment is an unavoidable expense for any dog owner. There is no National Health Service for pets, and the widow's mite dropping into the PDSA collection box is intended as a sacrifice to help the destitute, not the thrifty. Anyone taking a dog to the PDSA for treatment is asked to sign a declaration concerning his or her inability to pay for veterinary treatment elsewhere, and it costs an average £3.80 from the PDSA kitty to treat each pet they see (35,357 animals in 1986, for example). The British Veterinary Association and the British Small Animals Veterinary Association urge you to get your mongrel's health insured through one of the simple schemes now available. Consult your vet, or write to any of the following:

Pet Plan Ltd, 319–327 Chiswick High Road, London W4 4HH, tel: 01-995 1414
PAWS, Jardine Glanvill (UK) Ltd, Bristol and West House, 2 St Philips Place, Birmingham B3 2QG, tel: 021-236 9091.

Average current premiums are around £16–£30 per annum, there's *very* little red tape these days, and once your dog is insured, the vet's bill for a course of treatment, even for major surgery costing several hundred, should not exceed a few pounds. A mongrel with a broken leg can be just as painful to your budget as a pedigree with a broken leg, so do yourself a favour and take out some insurance. You may also consider the need for third-party insurance to protect you from liability for any damage or accident caused by your dog during its lifetime. Some general policies include provisions for your dog, but you can in any case get excellent third-party cover by joining either the National Canine Defence League (7.50 subscription, OAPs £3.45) or PRO Dogs (£10.00 subscription); *see* Appendix 6 for addresses and telephone numbers.

Preparing your home
What else will you need? Most vets and trainers would say an enclosed garden, please. It is possible to housetrain a dog in a flat, but this requires rather a lot of patience and ingenuity, use of a litter tray early on, followed by much running up and down stairs with your pet on a lead, sometimes in your night attire. If you have no pyjamas and live in a flat, consider a budgie.

A garden makes all your training work that much simpler. Fences must be secure; if there is a hole in the hedge, your mongrel will find it. Fence off any part of the garden where the dog must not go and cover fish ponds with wire netting. Check to see that gates shut properly and that an amorous dog can't squeeze underneath. Unfortunately, dogs can also dig and jump. A boxer or German shepherd dog can scale a seven-foot (2.1 m) fence and terriers are champion burrowers. Survey your garden carefully until you can see the measure of your dog's capabilities. If an emergency arises and you *must* leave your dog in the garden unattended for a short period while your fences are temporarily down, the RSPCA suggest as a last resort a 'running-chain' – attaching the dog's lead to a long wire or tough nylon cord overhead, so the dog has a little mobility; shade and water should be within reach. Please don't ever leave a dog chained up to a kennel or post. It is very cruel.

Indoors you will need a couple of dog bowls – earthenware are ideal for water as they don't tip over. The water bowl should be always available on the floor. The other bowl is for food – better than a plate because doggie noses push food over the edge and make a mess. Wash both regularly and thoroughly away from the family dishes. A safe dog-chewable toy, such as a cowhide bone, will be gratefully received and may save the furniture.

Finally, your dog will need a bed. For a little needle-toothed pup, always chewing, a cardboard box with an entrance cut out of one side and an old blanket or sweater in the bottom is quite adequate. For an adult, a handyman's wooden box, which can be scrubbed out periodically, is serviceable and cheap, so long as it has an entrance, something soft to lie on and wooden blocks to raise it a couple of inches off the floor out of draughts. Or else the popular rigid plastic bed answers the purpose very well. There are also very nice fibreglass beds on the market, if you can go to that expense, some with a gentle warming panel in the base – absolute luxury for dogs. In addition, there are folding pack-in-the-car beds, ideal for itinerant families, and a range of foam, furry and beanbag beds for the adult who can keep his teeth to himself. Choose a type that is washable, because dogs have parasites.

Whatever you choose, homemade or bought, you should place it in a corner away from draughts and paddling feet. This will be a refuge for your dog when he feels the world has 'gone to the humans'. All dogs love to sleep for a while during the day, and puppies need to snooze for long hours. The bed of a fully grown adult should be big enough to allow him to turn round and round before he settles, as dogs often do. I do not personally recommend wicker baskets, as they are draughty and tempting to chew, and a stray wicker in the bottom can give your mongrel a terrible surprise. Don't, by the way, let Mutley sleep on your bed. Apart from the parasite possibilities, dogs fidget in the night and stop your circulation by lying on you.

Bringing your new mongrel home, you will probably find that bedtime is the hardest part of the day, so it helps if there are comfortable sleeping quarters available. Pups and even bewildered adult newcomers who are obviously scared will appreciate a hot-water bottle well wrapped in an old towel to snuggle against. A stone hot water bottle may be safer than rubber because puppies are great chewers! Some breeders claim a ticking clock reminds the young puppy of his mother's heartbeat and helps him to nod off, though an alarm clock might have exactly the opposite effect! When you turn out the light and retire to bed, having praised the creature in its night box, there will be a short silence followed by whimpering and whining. Go downstairs and say *No!* very firmly. If it persists, you can either repeat the procedure or take dog and dogbed upstairs for a night or two. Vet David Coffey: 'It really is extremely severe to expect a puppy to settle down on its own in a new home in a strange bed amidst unusual smells without a "tear" or two. Take the poor thing to your bedroom for heaven's sake . . . Forget the nonsense you so often hear that, once it gets the idea of coming to your bedroom, you will never get it to sleep elsewhere.'[3] When your house is no longer weird and frightening, you will find your orphan will sleep anywhere in it, and not mind at all.

Outside kennels are not to be recommended for a companion animal intended to share your life, and some dogs' homes specifically ask you to keep their adoptees indoors. If a dog is not good enough to live in your house, perhaps it is not good enough for you altogether. Large, heavy-coated working dogs that are to be kept outside as guards need kennels constructed with weatherproof boarding, properly insulated, with roofing felt on the roof. Care should be taken that the kennel allows the animal room to stand, stretch and turn, and it should be raised a few inches out of the draught, facing away from the wind and shaded in summer. The best bedding is shredded paper (Shredabed or Dicebed), as straw may be infected with parasites or rat urine. Wood wool is good; newspaper is better than nothing. Bedding should be changed frequently and water always available just outside the kennel.

The first day

Don't expect too much; keep the proceedings low key. Show your newcomer his bed and his bowls – as suggested earlier, it is best to keep to the diet your dog has been used to for the first few days. Pups need three or four little snacks a day and you may offer some warm milk or cereal with a little added glucose or Lactol, but don't be surprised if there is no appetite at homecoming. Dog stomachs are queasy in a crisis and this *is* a crisis, for your mongrel if not for you. He thinks, 'Oh no, I've been farmed out to some more people now, and these will get rid of me tomorrow. Nobody wants a poor mongrel dog.' Be kind and gentle. Take several opportunities to say what a good dog he is. Imagine how you'd feel. Try to resist bunging a dogs'-home waif into a bath of hot water on the very first day, unless you have brought home a very amenable personality. Let the shock waves roll over him rather gradually. Show him the garden and say, 'Look what you've got!' He may never have seen grass and flowers before, let alone a tree. Memories of past thrashings will begin to fade; you may even discern a little wag struggling to express itself, though wags may be slow in coming. Try to ensure you're about the house all day on this special occasion. Think of it as your new dog's birthday, and take the day off work! Introduce the family without tumult or

fuss and be sure to let the newcomer sleep as much as he
wants. Sleep knits up the ravelled sleeve of care.

A name

Choose a name for your dog and stick to it, because this is a key
word for your pet to learn. If he or she arrives with a name
from the shelter that you can't stand, try to adapt it to some-
thing similar to avoid confusion. Many mongrel owners seem
to call their dogs by the standard half-dozen names; Jilly
Cooper's *Intelligent and Loyal* included acknowledgements to
22 Sallies, 15 Patches, 15 Sams and 14 Sandies, with 12 each of
Peters, Tobies and Judies. Well, really! What about Wallace,
Holly, Noah, Joss, Kate, Poppy, Tuffy, Dinsdale, Hattie,
Maud, Bosie, Butler, Madge, Blondie, Oswald, Peg, Baxter,
Dingo, Sidney, Sunny, Mo, Stanley, Geoffrey, Star, Chip, Pip,
Moll, Johnson, Merry, Harriet, Bitzy, Partly, Pinch, Cherry,
Oliver, Albert, Rupert, Fan, Tess, Effie, Polly, Marlon, Jethro,
Marshall, Meg, Oscar, Dot, Tray, Clark, Samwise, Bilbo
Baggins, Beanie, Twizzle, Brian, Be-Be, Bunty, Roland,
Heccie, Dan, Oona or Daisy Dumpling? Use your im-
agination.

Toilet training

You should begin toilet training on Day One. Pups are little
orphans – orphan wetting and orphan messing. They sleep a
lot and have frequent meals, and a puppy under three months
has no more control over rear-end mysteries than a human
baby. When it wakes up and after meals, or when it shows signs
of wanting to relieve itself (you'll soon notice what these are),
pick the pup up, put it down gently in the garden and when it
wets or defecates say 'Garden!' and praise it lavishly. It will
then associate the word 'garden' with the toilet, and with much
patience you can trigger the bodily function by using the
sound, in the same way that Pavlov caused dogs to salivate to
the sound of tuning forks. 'Garden' is the place where your
dog's natural functions will cause least offence to the dainty
British public.

   Indoors and at night, you will need some newspaper. A pup

Bundle – Scruffts 1984 Supreme Champion

Samantha, the duck dog

Bugsy Malone and Lindsay – the first Scruffts Supreme Champion in 1983 was in fact not a mongrel at all…

A leading Scruffts contender 1984, waiting to enter the Lamp-post User section

Above   Overlooked in the rescue kennels for
five months, Kahla now plays cricket and
hockey and pinches children's shoes

Right   Tina at home in Battersea

Right   Battersea Blackie in his prize-
winning days

Below   Bambi – 'can jump any height'

Landseer's 'Highland Dogs'. Notice how pedigrees were once rough and ready

Feral dogs running wild in America

will not usually soil his own bed and will prefer newspaper to a cold floor. Over a period of time, move the newspaper zone nearer and nearer the back door until finally, as the puppy watches, you place it just outside. This will make the 'Garden' transition easier for it to understand, and eventually you'll find the creature at the back door when nature calls. Do let it out promptly, even if you're busy, or you may have to go back to square one. There will be errors. Clear them up with a little disinfectant and spray the spot with deodorant.

Housetraining may take several weeks or even months. Scold the dog when it makes a mistake, putting it immediately in the garden, but don't rub its nose in the puddle: to an animal with such a highly developed scenting capability, this is very cruel. If you catch the miscreant in the very act, noise is the best rebuff. Slap a newspaper in your hand or bang an old tin tray. Don't punish the dog for an 'old' puddle. He has no knowledge of history and will think he is being scolded for his present behaviour – which may be the greeting he gives you when you come in from the shops. Remember, dogs learn by association, not 'morals'.

A dogs'-home adult waif that has not been housetrained at all is less common than one that has lapsed through being shut in kennels. In any case, you should use exactly the same methods as for a pup and persevere. 'Garden' first thing in the morning, last thing at night, and after meals. Lavish praise when it does its stuff, repeating the word 'garden' till it sounds to you like gobbledegook. Have patience. Don't lecture the dog. One sound, however monotonous to you, is easier for him to remember; the Guide Dog Association use the word 'busy'. Don't blame the dog for incompetence. An adult mongrel accustomed to roaming the streets before he met you has no experience of bowel or bladder control. He may take a long time – months even – to get his degree in potty science, just like a puppy, and an adult male's problem is compounded by the fact that he cocks his leg against the vertical to trigger urination, which if he is shut indoors may mean one of your walls or a piece of furniture. If you have particular problems like this, your vet may be able to help, as there are drugs to suppress male hormone 'marking' in the house. Otherwise try the simple expedient of putting the dog's bed in a room with a tiled or linoleum surface and newspaper, as for puppies, and restricting the area at night by means of a 'pen'. Feed the dog at regular times and it will generally defecate at regular times. Avoid feeding him late at night. Flat-dwellers with either a pup or an adult will need a cat-litter tray, again moved gradually nearer the door. When you're about to give up hope, lift up your eyes unto the hills – hundreds of thousands of foster-owners *succeed* and if they can do it, so can you.

While you're in the garden, you can practise potty-training on the lead, because once your pet's vaccination programme is complete, you can take him for a proper walk. Please don't let him defecate on the footpath – it stirs up dog hatred. If you see signs of him preparing to relieve himself – urgent scratching, circling or squatting – hurry him to the kerb and say 'Garden!' ('Garden' is a good word to say in public – better than some of the alternatives! Don't, by the way, just say, 'Good boy!' or 'Good girl!' Otherwise whenever you say this, the dog will think you mean 'go to the lavatory'.) Avoid children's playing fields even though your dog has been wormed. Ask your local council to provide a dog loo or waste patch. They can, you know, and should, if they place strictures on dogs in parks. You are a ratepayer and you are entitled to take your dog somewhere. Dogs, you can tell them, prefer grass to any other surface, if they'd be so kind.

There is another sort of 'toilet' problem – spraying. Some dogs and some bitches 'spray' when they are very excited, such as when they are thrilled you've come home. Don't smack the dog – it can't help it, and it may have been trying to control itself with a full bladder. Take it into the garden for now, and consult your veterinary surgeon.

Obedience

Mongrels are quite *capable* of a high level of obedience training. Barbara Woodhouse told me, 'Mongrels react in exactly the same way as purebred dogs. Overseas I train 99 per cent of mongrels in my TV work, from the animal shelters, always hoping they will get homes after people have seen how well they work.' During the war, ex-strays were trained as sentries and messengers, upon whom men's lives depended, and mongrels and crossbreeds have turned out as Guide Dogs and Hearing Dogs for the Deaf – you can't get more highly trained than that.

Of course, mongrels *are* more independent and intelligent than pedigree clones, which means that schooling must be presented as an interesting challenge if they are not to find it beneath their dignity. The fact is that many of us adopt mongrels precisely *because* they are wayward and eccentric, and we are faintly appalled at the sight of pedigrees square-bashing and jumping through hoops. My own mongrel Stanley simply would not stand for it and, if he sees such regimental coves on television, threatens to set about the lot of them for being traitors to dogkind. For most mongrel owners, I would suggest, there is a happy medium between the dog despot mentioned earlier and the fur soldier, and that is the sort of pet who obeys the law and the house rules and who comes (eventually) when called. This is the level of training I would aim for, although of course it's entirely up to you and your dog.

There are over 500 training clubs in the UK whose addresses can be obtained from the Kennel Club (*see* Appendix 6 for address and telephone number). These clubs generally accept any dog – mongrel or pedigree – over six months of age, though if you have a puppy, you should be teaching the rudiments beforehand yourself, not letting him run delinquent. Go along to a club and have a look. If you see dogs being literally throttled with choke chains or, worse still, beaten and teased by people in padded sleeves, think very carefully indeed about enrolling your friend, especially if you think he or she may have been ill-treated. I have heard of tragic cases of dogs that have become savage after physical-coercion training. Classes of the right sort can be an invaluable help: what they do is to school the owner in basic confidence at dog-handling so that you can go away and train the dog yourself.

The first requirement of all obedience training is to get your dog used to the collar and lead. Pup or adult, it makes no difference: it must get used to this equipment to live in our overcrowded country and it is an offence to walk a dog along a designated highway *without* a collar, tag and lead. If you adopt an adult, it may well have worn them before; a puppy will find it all very strange. Put the collar on in the house for brief periods for a few days and go about your business. Ignore the rebellion; he will soon get used to it provided the collar is not too tight (two-finger room). Mother hippos train their babies to swim by knocking them off the bank and letting them get on with it and, by and large, animals make much less fussy parents than we do. That's the first lesson. All the other lessons are based on the principle: demonstrate, repeat, reward. The worst enemy of anyone trying to train a dog is confusion, so be clear at every stage. Have one person teaching the dog, not half a dozen. Few words, simple sounds that will make the association in the dog's mind, then lots of praise because mongrels don't hear very much of that in this world.

'No'

You can usually stop a dog *in flagrante delicto* by making a loud noise. Say 'No! *No!*' loudly and harshly, dropping the pitch of your voice if you can. A metal tray banged against the wall makes a good accompaniment, which is very mysterious and alarming to a dog, and when it associates the act with the racket, it will desist. My dog responds instantly to the threat of 'Where's that tray!' without ever having felt the caress of it in his life. The famous German service dog trainer Konrad Most, although *he* used physical coercion as well, found the word 'Bah!' very effective. Smacking, on the other hand, is generally *in*effective. The safe area to hit a dog, on the rump, is not as vulnerable as a child's bottom, and if the dog doesn't actually snap at you, he probably didn't feel anything anyway. *Never* hit a dog on the head or the snout, and never bash a little puppy. If you must go to extremes, use a bitch's method of shaking him by the scruff of his neck. At least he will understand what you're doing.

The lead

A quick jerk on the lead is an effective form of training – better than smacks, sticks or rolled-up newspapers, all of which keep the dog out of range and repel it from you. Training requires close contact, and there is no point in ordering a dog to do something if you're not in a position to enforce it. The lead is your hot line to your dog's brain. Get a pup used to wearing one by clipping it gently to his collar in the house and letting him run up and down under your supervision (keep an eye on him as the lead may catch on something). Chewing can be deterred by dabbing paraffin on the leather. The next step is to hold the lead at arm's length, backing away and proffering a titbit, which will introduce the queer (to a dog) 'lead feeling' without wrenching the animal up and down. Keep the lessons short and sweet. An adult mongrel unused to a lead may be introduced in the same way, but have his lessons in the garden where he can buck without breaking anything. Don't be exasperated because you think these are rudimentary 'puppy' lessons for a grown dog. It may be completely new to him.

The alternative to the choke chain, Dr Mugford's Halti (*see* p. 51), comes with fitting and teaching instructions and is worn round the dog's head like a halter, with the lead attached. This, too, takes some getting used to, and should be tried out in the garden, with the dog running up and down on the lead until he forgets his indignation. There is also a leather slip collar, available from most good pet shops, that will control a big dog more kindly than a choke chain, if you are really stuck.

Heel

Stand your dog on your left, lead in your right hand across your body. Hustle the dog firmly up and down, talking to him merrily. If he won't budge, use a titbit as an interim measure (but don't go mad with titbits or you'll have a fat dog). If he pulls ahead, which is much more likely, give a jerk on his collar and say 'Heel!' There's no need to wrench the dog over in a backward somersault; you'll find that if you walk briskly and make a lot of right turns, you'll automatically be in the driving seat and he'll have to pay attention to your movements. These should be short lessons, but you may have to repeat them over and over again because it is quite hard for a mongrel to get into his head that he must keep pace with a human. Some mongrels never can be bothered with precision heelwork because they get bored, but so long as you can train the dog not to drag you to destruction, you have achieved the main object of the exercise. For a big, burly customer with no sense at all, consider a Halti.

Sit

Even the most dominant, unreclaimed adult mongrel relies on you for his food, and you should use this to demonstrate your authority. At mealtimes, hold the dog's bowl in one hand above his nose and command him to 'Sit!' Say it as though you mean it. If you have him backing away with his rear end facing a wall, he will feel physically inclined to sit down anyway; otherwise use your free hand to show him what you mean, pressing down firmly on his hindquarters near the tail. No sit, no din-dins. Be firm. The food method of teaching the 'sit' is better than the lead method, pulling the dog's head up, because it offers a real reward. Pups are fed three or four times a day, so you will have plenty of practice at instilling your authority.

Stay

This is a continuation of the 'sit', reinforced with a hand signal. If the dog gets up, make him sit down again and say 'Sit – stay!' very firmly. This is not 'teasing' the dog but capturing his entire attention at the moment when you have most natural control over him – as his dinner-giver. It establishes in his mind that you are the giver of good things and must be listened to, and if you make it a daily routine, the dog will begin to obey you in other ways.

Dogs left alone

Many dogs start barking and gnawing when left on their own, and some dogs that have ended up in shelters have been evicted by their owners for this very reason. A mongrel should be perfectly all right on his own for three or four hours while you go out, provided he has water to drink and a cowhide bone to chew, and provided you have taken a tiny bit of trouble over his training. The method is simple. After he has gone to the toilet, calmly put the dog or pup in another room and shut the door. Go about your business, but listen for sounds of showing off or destruction. If there's a racket, bang loudly on the door and shout 'Ugh! Bad dog!' and if necessary make a great show of thundering in the room and shaming the treachery. The first lesson might last five minutes, the next ten and so on. Work up gradually until you can leave the animal on his own for a couple of hours with complete confidence. This is training without tears, because the dog will resign himself to your absence and very probably go to sleep.

As a general rule, *over*-attachment and possessiveness will inevitably cause problems in an owner's relationship with a dog, so love him devotedly but try not to become a clinging couple. Clinging dogs make their own lives a misery and feel so lonely when left that they will defecate, drink out of the toilet bowl, tear, gnaw and howl to show you their feelings. Avoid such habits by the behind-closed-door technique. If you can't face the discipline involved, have two dogs, rather than one. Then they can cling desperately to each other when you go out for five minutes.

Down – Stay

Once your dog has learned to 'sit' and 'stay' for his dinner, he will sit on command on the lead and he will know that 'stay' means to keep still. If you wish to extend his repertoire, you can now teach him 'down', which is fairly easy. From the sit position, casually pull his forelegs from under him so that he is lying instead of sitting, and say 'Down – stay!' Repeat it a few times – he may keep getting up, and be lavish with your praise when he obeys you. Reinforce the 'stay' by attaching a Flexi-lead or training cord to your dog's collar and backing away with your palm extended, increasing the distance little by little and returning to praise him profusely if he remains down. Once you're sure he's steady, you can throw caution to the wind and try it without any lead at all, preferably in the garden at first, in case he's crafty.

Come

In this lesson, rather than you returning to the dog, your dog comes to you. With your mutt on the long lead, walk away from him quietly and when you reach the extent of the lead, turn and face him. Call his name, say 'Come!' in a delighted cheerful voice, and give a friendly tug on the lead if he needs any encouragement. When he reaches you, praise, laud and honour him because this is a wonderful thing for a dog to learn. Always bend down to praise him – don't let him jump up, not even a little puppy. Jumping can injure children and elderly people and the habit usually sets in because the dog has been encouraged to leap into someone's arms as a pup. Forewarned is forearmed. You should practise 'come', 'down' and 'stay' many times on the extended lead before you practise without it, or free. The 'come' requires great patience, and lessons should always take place well away from traffic or livestock. If the dog takes ages to come to you, don't smack or scold him when he finally obeys. This will make the association in the dog's mind of 'come – wallop' instead of 'come – glad'. The *usual* response to a refusal to come should not be to chase the dog or try to stalk up on it, but to turn on your heels and start to walk away.

That's more or less the Green Cross Code for mongrels. Why do more? Dr Roger Mugford, animal behaviourist: 'I'm not out for perfection. All I'm out for is happy relationships, and nobody getting bitten anymore. Dogs are very proficient at reading our body language, and they have a central processing capacity that is not as great as ours but certainly in a very high league. We're constantly underestimating them by such nonsense as expecting them to sit because we put a special emphasis on the "t" – "*si-tttt!*" It's all bizarre. The majority of dogs form very satisfactory habits and adequate relationships with their owners simply on the basis of a non-interference policy. You train the minimum, of coming when you say *come*, heeling and sitting when you say *heel* and *sit*, staying when you say *stay*, and possibly going down when you say *down* – and that's it. A basic easy framework, and then the rest is just a nice, developing relationship.'

Of problem dogs, on which Dr Mugford is an acknowledged expert, he has this to say as a general tip: 'Training classes which overemphasize the need for physical and mental domination, as a master with his slave, leave a lot of dog owners reeling with shock at what they see and hear and are expected to do. Some ex-Forces trainer tells them, "You've gotta dominate your dog and this is how you do it! You put the choker on it and when it does the wrong thing, you go like *this* and you show it 'oo's boss. Right? Now *you* do it!" There *are* puppy clubs in the Home Counties, which is the area I happen to know, run on totally different lines, and which are very good.'

You can do a great deal, though, at home, by remembering that the dog is dependent on you for food, shelter and affection. Says Dr Mugford: 'Love the dog, but realize that this attachment is also a potent weapon, and that you can manipulate this variable to your own and your pet's advantage. People who come to me with their problem dogs find it strange that my asking them to do nothing can be as potent as my asking them to do *something*.' This is why, if your dog refuses to come, the best response is usually not to chase after it, but to turn and start walking away. A dog's need to be loved is greater than its fear of chastisement. Diversion is better than whacking. Holding the food bowl in the air is better than a military campaign. You have the greatest conceivable advantage over your dog – your brain. You don't need to go fifteen rounds with him.

5

Exercise, health and care

We begin this chapter with the subject of the Great Outdoors, because the responsibilities entailed are terribly important for any dog owner, and for the mongrel owner, they are binding. We need to make a special effort for the True Dog, in view of what has happened in the past.

The great outdoors

All dogs need daily exercise for their physical and mental well-being. Obesity, lack of exercise and boredom account for a very high proportion of canine casualties with avoidable health and behavioural problems. Arthritis, diabetes and many other diseases in dogs have been linked to excess fat. Veterinary surgeon Tony Cowie: 'We spend an awful lot of time slimming dogs with premature arthritis, premature heart problems, too much fat in the abdomen around the liver and kidneys causing dysfunction, and dogs with a massive two-inch-thick shell of fat around them, pulling themselves to pieces because they get so hot.' Chewing, dirtiness, barking and aggressive tendencies may all develop from the boredom and frustration of an under-exercised dog. Just how *much* exercise they need is debatable. Some authorities say a dog the size of a German shepherd needs as much as one-and-a-half hours daily off the lead, and one the size of a labrador needs one hour running plus access to a large garden. A King Charles spaniel-size dog needs forty minutes and a Yorkie-size needs three-quarters of an hour split into short walks, according to the same experts.[1] Dogs also need to run, jump or swim, like animals in the wild. There's nothing to prevent you putting a little obstacle course in your back garden, and most canines appreciate a game of 'fetch' or 'tug'. If you can't walk your mongrel to some safe 'free run' outside, then a brisk pace on the lead is better than a dawdle, and running is better still. Remember, the Canidae family evolved as tireless toe-walkers capable of marathons. They weren't made for pottering about indoors all day long. Be careful, though, not to overtire elderly dogs and puppies. Don't go too far in roasting heat with any mongrel, and if it's a filthy day, dry him off with an old towel when he comes in.

Dog-stealing

Mongrel owners are famous for keeping latch-key dogs that are put out in the morning and let in at night, rather like a cat only the other way around. This solves the problem of exercise, certainly, so why shouldn't you do it? Firstly, because it is illegal and anti-social, and secondly, because if you let your mongrel out on the streets alone, there is a very good chance that you will never see him again. Apart from any traffic accidents he may be involved in (for which the owner, incidentally, is liable), and apart from the authorities being likely to pick him up for vagrancy, there is a rife trade in pet-stealing in Britain that, like other cash-related crimes, is on the increase.

Some dogs that go missing have not wandered off, or been picked up by sympathetic bystanders. Some have simply been stolen, from gardens, cars, shop doorways. Why would anyone want to steal a dog, particularly if it happens to be a down-market mongrel? Because the thieves can sell them to vivisection laboratories, dealers, the dog-fight trade. They don't have to be pedigrees. Brian Gunn, former General Secretary of the National Anti-Vivisection Society (NAVS), showed me documents and photographs relating to mongrels just like yours being used as vivisectors' tools in UK laboratories. One internal laboratory document, which found its way into the possession of the NAVS, is an application for six dogs to be used in a particular research project, carrying the approval, 'OK to proceed, but please use the term "nonaccredited", not "mongrels".' This is because dogs purpose-bred for laboratory research are pedigrees, normally beagles or labradors, and the presence of mongrels would be potentially embarrassing to the laboratory concerned.

Vivisection runners operate all over the country. Said Brian Gunn, 'There are unfortunately so many surplus and unwanted dogs about, particularly so in 1984 for economic reasons. Stolen pets are docile and very easy for thieves and laboratory technicians to handle, and strays that are obviously hungry can be lured with food into a van. The thieves will also use a bitch on heat to lure stray male dogs. These sort of people don't see the animal as a dog, a living, sentient, individual being. They see it as X pounds, and they regard stealing it as rather like stealing something from a supermarket. They scour the newspapers and pet-shop windows for unwanted dogs – it's a cheap supply because the owners are usually so relieved to think that the dog is going to a decent home, they will give it to the thieves free of charge. Of course, the person who actually obtains the dog is not the same fellow who sells it to the laboratory because the vivisectors are very careful as to whom they deal with. There's usually a "fence", a so-called respectable middle-man. A mongrel stolen in London would probably be used in a laboratory as far away as Bristol. It's all very well organized.'

The laboratories under the greatest financial pressure to use stolen dogs are the ones shortest of money, like the medical schools and universities that can't afford too many legal beagles. Brian Gunn showed me a current catalogue from *Interfauna*, approved breeders of laboratory animals, offering beagles for research at the going rates: 'Beagles from 3–4 months, £175 each; 4–5 months, £190 each; 5–6 months, £210 each; 6–7 months, £230 each; 7–8 months, £245 each; 8–9 months, £260 each; over 9 months, ask for special quotations.'

'This is where,' says Brian Gunn, 'pet-stealing comes very much into the frame. Although the number of experiments on animals in general is falling, the number performed on dogs is higher than at any time since 1977.'

Figures issued by the Home Office for 1987 show that

12,901 dogs were used, some had anaesthetic for part of the experiment but 6812 had no anaesthetic.[2] Over 3 million (3,112,051) experiments were performed on living animals in Britain in 1987 to test everything from mascara through weapons to crack-brained psychological theories, and although the statistical trend is down, this is no comfort to the animals being used, as each one can only feel its own pain. The NAVS warn, 'Never let your pet out alone; be suspicious of strangers approaching your pets or neighbours' animals. A £500 reward is offered by the National Anti-Vivisection Society to anyone supplying information leading to the conviction of any person caught stealing and supplying animals for vivisection.' (For further information contact the NAVS: *see* Appendix 6 for address and telephone number.)

The case for keeping your dog where you can see him is summed up by the following newspaper cutting, reporting on recent court proceedings:

> ... Mr McGill said afterwards that he had been a dog dealer for fifteen years and had sold some of his animals to laboratories. He bought them from other dealers and kennels, but declined to name his sources or any of the research centres he supplied. Mr McGill added, 'They are unwanted dogs. The streets are full of them. You can go to any of the dogs' homes and see them. I have got a living to make. I sell them to anybody. I cannot live on sentiment.'[3]

Please walk your mongrel. Don't leave him to his fate.

The British Union for the Abolition of Vivisection comment in their campaigning newspaper the *Liberator*:

> In the past five years there has been continuous evidence of non-purpose-bred dogs being used in Government-funded laboratories such as universities and those associated with hospitals. From the dogs rescued by NALL [Northern Animal Liberation League] on the Sheffield University raid in 1981 to those rescued by the ALF [Animal Liberation Front] from Laundry Farm, Cambridge, to the dogs photographed by SEALL [South East Animal Liberation League] at the RCS [Royal College of Surgeons] so recently, there is one long line of animals whose breeds range from Alsatians to Rhodesian ridgebacks, from spaniels to Old English sheepdogs, plus a multitude of mongrels and crossbreeds, all of which were

obviously former pets – dogs that knew how to fetch sticks and sit and walk on command.

The Government has made feeble attempts in The Animals (Scientific Procedures) Bill to allay public concern by the insertion of the following words: 'The use of dogs or cats found straying will not be permitted.' Such words are meaningless when unscrupulous suppliers sign forms to the effect that the animals they sell to the laboratories are their own property.

The dealers in this sickening trade are beneath contempt. But no trade can exist without a demand. It is those who demand these animals for their immoral experiments who create this trade, and it is the Government who deny and conveniently turn a blind eye to its existence who allow it to continue.

Travel and travel sickness

Long journeys by car or public transport are no problem so long as your dog has been gradually acclimatized to them. Dogs are carried upstairs on buses at the discretion of the conductor, and ride in trains at child fare, although it is advisable to travel at off-peak hours, otherwise you may end up sitting with your charge in a corridor. Despite your dog being better behaved and a lot cleaner than many children, he will not be permitted on the seats. For the fortunate car-owner, journeys are easier, but try not to make the dog's first experience of travel a trip to the vet, to be stuck with sharp spines or given bad grits, or whatever other interpretation dogs put on veterinary surgeries – they don't seem to like them much. Your dog should travel in the back of the car, away from the driver's controls, ideally behind an estate-car dog-guard. If you *must* leave him alone in the vehicle, please park in the shade in summer and come back periodically to check that he's OK. The window should be rolled down a little for adequate ventilation. Dogs have died *in* cars, as well as under them.

Most enjoy car journeys; others have to be introduced gradually to the joys of motoring. Accustom your puppy or rescue dog by taking it round the block a few times, and if this doesn't calm its fears, try feeding it in the car, or playing with it in the back while the car is stationary. You can desensitize a dog to motion-sickness, salivating and panic in the same way with a little patience, turning the engine on and off and teaching the animal that a car is not a death cell but an extension of your home. It will soon get the idea. Take the rug or blanket out of his bed and put it in the car, and on long journeys always carry a plastic water bottle and his bowl in case he gets thirsty, allowing for toilet stops along the way. Once your dog can travel happily you can take him on holiday trips with you; he will sleep in the car and save you kennelling costs.

Travel sickness can often be helped by the dog taking a heaped teaspoonful of glucose powder in two tablespoons of water before the journey and further doses of the same *en route* (more for a larger dog). Never feed him just before you travel, and if motion sickness is a persistent problem, consult your vet. Tony Cowie: 'Puppies get a lot of travel sickness; when they come in for their first vaccination, they arrive slobbering and salivating and they've often brought up their dinner in the back of the car. You can get a puppy used to cars by taking it on little journeys to the shops. Then there's travel *nuisance* – the dog that leaps and bounces around in the back of the car when you've got to go to the north of Scotland, and he barks when he sees other dogs and other cars and messes in the corner and your journey's hell before you've done two miles. There are super little inexpensive travel-sickness pills that you can get from the vet: they're tranquillizers but they're also designed to suppress vomiting and generally calm the animal down.' These are not, however, recommended for the short-haul journey; in that case, try the glucose trick or ask your vet about prescribing a children's travel-sickness pill.

Diet

All dogs need adequate supplies of protein, fats, carbo-hydrates and roughage, vitamins, minerals and water. Unfortunately, diet for dogs is a very controversial subject and no two of the numerous authorities I consulted wholly agreed on what you should give your mongrel to keep it in the pink. I was led through a maze of alimentary canals past kilocals, Meaty Mash, Bouncy Bits and a good deal of rubbish. According to some 'experts', my own dogs, which subsist largely on fresh cooked meat and run gleaming over the landscape, should be dead, and much of the advice on balanced scientifically prepared foods came from people with vested interests in marketing balanced scientifically prepared foods.

So one cannot be too dogmatic about your dog's dinner, but the following, at least, is true. Dogs are carnivores and their teeth are designed as carnivore cutlery. In the wild, they eat flesh, bone and offal as well as the contents of their victims' stomachs that contain some vegetable matter. If necessary, dogs will drop down the food chain and become omnivorous (unlike cats), eating vegetables, fruit, berries and reptiles, and the suburban red fox is known to subsist at certain times of year on earthworms and little else. But these are adaptations of the norm. Given the choice, dogs will eat meat in preference to other foodstuffs, and they will eat it high and putrid too, because they have a resistance to bacteria in putrefying flesh. The habit of grass-eating, observed in many domestic dogs, is not really a dietary requirement, but grass is a handy emetic for bringing up fur and bone that might otherwise become lodged in the dog's stomach.

Bones, especially of the splintering sort (poultry and rabbit bones break up into sharp needles), may indeed get stuck in the dog's digestive tract and vets do have to remove them surgically. Conversely, dogs love a bone, and bones contain important nutrients and may help to scale off calculus from the teeth. Beef shank marrow bones – the big ones – are probably the best to gnaw and will not splinter; they should be blanched to kill the germs but not cooked, as this makes them brittle. If your mongrel is a huge fellow with powerful jaws, though, caution is advised because big dogs have been known to pulverize even marrow bones into a sort of cement that sets in their guts. I leave the decision to you. If you are worried about bones, you can buy bone flour instead, but make sure it is the sterilized sort. I pass on to you the informed opinion of at least one veterinary surgeon, R. C. G. Hancock, who has a bone to pick with those who advise against any bones at all: 'In a healthy animal not too degenerated by human malpractice in breeding, the gastric juice contains sufficient hydrochloric acid to soften bone and release the soluble lime salts the body needs . . .'4

If you like the idea of a traditional diet for your dog, you should think in terms of inexpensive cuts and butchers' pet mince, balanced with white meat and fish, and offal such as liver for variety and nutrients. Too much offal may cause diarrhoea; once or twice a week sits well with most dogs. You may supplement this meaty diet with cow's-milk (provided that your dog is not allergic like some pedigrees and pooftas), toasted bread, potatoes and, according to *some* authorities, though not all, vitamins and minerals, strictly according to the dosage on the pack. Beware of overdosing your dog, or yourself, with vitamins. Bone dystrophies and other mal-functions are known to result from vitamin poisoning, and dogs do not, ever, require vitamin C – they manufacture it themselves. My own view is that, provided a dog has a variety of nourishing meats as the basis of his diet, you can chuck the vitamin supplements in the bin. My dogs have never needed them. Eggs, if you feed them to your mongrel, should be cooked, as raw egg white contains a substance that could cause a biotin deficiency and subsequent hair loss and doggie dandruff. Raw meat, the dog diet in the wild, is not a good idea for a domesticated dog because of lost resistance to bacteria. Again, this is up to you, but if you buy pet meat or condemned meat, you are feeding bugs to your mongrel's unsuspecting stomach. And although it is impossible to prove any connection between raw meat and aggression, there are stories, bloodcurdling tales of dogs run wild and torn carotid arteries . . . Why not put it on the stove and sleep nights?

The alternative to the traditional cooked-meat diet is to choose one of the less expensive varieties – the offal-based diet, tinned meat, the 'expanded meal' diet and the 'soft-moist' diet. The expanded meal and soft-moist types are generally complete foods and need nothing added (please read the packet). The other two *need balancing* by adding biscuit meal. Whichever you choose, and the French have published a 500-page recipe book for pets if your dog is something of a gourmet, please do *not*, repeat *not*, feed your dog on leftovers and titbits. You will lose control over his health and you will very probably end up with a fat dog. Obese dogs have shorter lives. Some dogs *are* finicky and have to be tempted; others will get in next-door's dustbin given half a chance. All mongrels have ancestral memories of starvation, and may respond by salting away food caches and bones 'for later', or for a rainy day. Many dispense with the formalities of burial or hidden hoards and simply store their supplies in fat, just in case, and as long as there is food in front of them, they will gobble. This is not hunger, but insecurity.

Watch your dog's weight: if you can lift him, you can stand on the bathroom scales with him and then simply subtract what you weigh yourself. Dogs should have a waist, and you should be able to feel ribs though not see them. If you have a fatty or a skinny, consult your vet, and stick to the regime he or she prescribes, without cheating. Take no notice of the eyes like tinderboxes at the oven door: you are being more cruel if you give in. Try to give your dog his meals at regular times, so that he really does know where his next meal is coming from, and although dogs tend to eat more in cold weather and after exertion, note any radical changes in appetite as a possible sign of disease. Any change in *diet* should be made gradually over a period of days. Dog stomachs are inclined to react badly to different menus served without warning. Finally, don't forget the water. Fresh water should be always available in the bowl. Dogs can't turn on taps.

If you plan to feed convenience foods, fine – they are an economic way of ensuring your dog gets all the nutrients he requires without too much weighing and mashing. Always read the manufacturers' instructions carefully though, because different products are prepared for different purposes, and not all packages and tins are intended to suffice as a complete diet. Which brand? I personally would hesitate to buy my mongrel a product marketed under the name of Clone Chum, though of course the dietary requirements for both mongrels and pedigrees are the same. I dislike any suggestion that mongrels are undesirable or unsaleable, and believe that snob-value advertising reaffirms popular misconceptions about mongrels and leads to more uncaring ownership.

I put it to Eric Smethurst of Pedigree Petfoods, who do so

much valuable research into dog care and welfare in other fields, that perhaps his company don't want mongrels to eat their products. 'There couldn't be anything further from the truth,' he said. 'Mongrels have absolutely the same needs as pedigree dogs and our brands – Bounce, Chappie, Mr Dog, Pal, Pedigree Chum, Frolic and Mick are available in every shop in the land. We believe we feed practically every dog in the country one way or another. Pedigree Petfoods is just the name of the *company*.' Oh really. Jon Delap of Spillers, on the other hand, told me, 'There's absolutely no difference between the requirements of a pedigree and a mongrel. The requirements are calculated scientifically: a dog of X weight needs so many kilocals to go about his business, depending on the degree of exercise, and a working mongrel will obviously need more kilocals than a sedentary pet. Slightly amusing in *our* research, though is that owners who feed their dogs on Pedigree Petfoods seem to have more rascally behaved dogs!' Oh really?

Whichever diet you choose for your True Dog, there are no rigid rules as to quantity because dogs vary in their metabolism just like humans. But the following charts, reprinted with permission, should help you gauge roughly what to give.

Chart 1[5]

Weight of dog	20 lb (9 kg)	40 lb (18 kg)	65 lb (29.5 kg)
Typical breed	*Corgi, stand. dachshund*	*Welsh springer, bull terrier*	*Boxer, retriever, setter*
Kcal needed	700	1100	1600
1. Traditional	5 oz (140 g) minced beef ¼ lb (115 g) wholemeal bread 2 fl. oz (55 ml) cow's-milk Vitamin/mineral concentrate as instructed on pack	½ lb (225 g) minced beef 7 oz (200 g) wholemeal bread Vitamin/mineral concentrate as instructed on pack	¾ lb (340 g) minced beef 10 oz (285 g) wholemeal bread Vitamin/mineral concentrate as instructed on pack
2. Offal and biscuits	¾ lb (340 g) stewed tripe	1 lb (455 g) stewed tripe	1¼ lb (565 g) stewed tripe

	2 oz (60 g) ox liver 3 oz (85 g) dog biscuits ¼ oz (7 g) bone flour	2 oz (60 g) ox liver 6 oz (170 g) dog biscuits ⅓ oz (10 g) bone flour	2 oz (60 g) ox liver 10 oz (285 g) dog biscuits ½ oz (15 g) bone flour
3. Tinned meat and biscuit meal	½ can (7 oz, 200 g) 'meat-in-jelly' 5 oz (140 g) biscuit meal	¾ can (10½ oz, 300 g) 'meat-in-jelly' 8½ oz (240 g) biscuit meal	1 can (14 oz, 395 g) 'meat and cereal' ¾ lb (340 g) biscuit meal
4. Expanded meal (balanced diet)	7½ oz (215 g)	¾ lb (340 g)	17 oz (480 g)
5. Soft-moist (balanced diet)	8½ oz (240 g)	13 oz (370 g)	19½ oz (555 g)

The chart suggests four different types of diet and gives average quantities for dogs of 20, 40 and 65 lb body weight during their middle years. The following notes should be read in conjunction with the chart.

(i)   The quantities suggested are only a *guide* because of individual variation.

(ii) The fat content of some foods varies, particularly fresh meat and offals, and this can greatly affect their energy value.

Chart 2[6]

Weight of dog	20 lb (9 kg)	40 lb (18 kg)	60 lb (27 kg)
Example breed	*Corgi*	*Springer spaniel*	*Boxer, Irish setter*
Home-made diet	5 oz (140 g) beef ¼ lb (115 g) wholemeal bread 2 fl oz (55 ml) milk Vitamins Minerals	½ lb (225 g) beef ½ lb (225 g) wholemeal bread Vitamins Minerals	¾ lb (340 g) beef 10 oz (285 g) wholemeal bread Vitamins Minerals

Canned meat	½ can (7 oz, 200 g) of meaty food	¾ can (10½ oz, 300 g) of meaty food	1 can (14 oz, 395 g) of meaty food
Plus biscuit	5 oz (140 g) biscuit	8½ oz (240 g) biscuit	¾ lb (340 g) biscuit

Chart 3[7]

Daily ration

Weight of dog	22 lb (10 kg)	45 lb (20 kg)	65 lb (30 kg)
1. OFFAL AND BISCUIT			
Stewed tripe	13½ oz (380 g)	1.1 lb (500 g)	1¼ lb (600 g)
Ox liver	2¼ oz (65 g)	2¼ oz (65 g)	2¼ oz (65 g)
Dog biscuits	3¼ oz (95 g)	7 oz (190 g)	10 oz (300 g)
Sterilized bone flour	¼ oz (8 g)	⅓ oz (10 g)	½ oz (15 g)
2. COOKED FRESH MEAT			
Chopped/minced beef	5½ oz (160 g)	9 oz (250 g)	¾ lb (350 g)
Wholemeal bread	4½ oz (130 g)	7 oz (200 g)	10 oz (300 g)
Milk	2 fl. oz (60 ml)	3 fl. oz (90 ml)	6 fl. oz (180 ml)
Vitamin mineral supplement	see recommended inclusion rates on carton		
3. EXPANDED MEALS (complete food)	9 oz (240 g)	14 oz (385 g)	1 lb (500 g)
4. SOFT MOIST FOOD (complete food)	10 oz (270 g)	15 oz (420 g)	1 lb 2 oz (570 g)
5. CANNED MEAT AND BISCUIT			
Meat/jelly type	½ lb (225 g)	11 oz (335 g)	1 lb (500 g)
Biscuit meal	5½ oz (160 g)	10 oz (270 g)	¾ lb (350 g)
6. MEAT/CEREAL AND BISCUIT			
Canned meat/cereal	7 oz (200 g)	10 oz (300 g)	14½ oz (400 g)
Biscuit meal	5 oz (150 g)	9 oz (250 g)	¾ lb (350 g)

Feeding puppies

In the wild the nursing bitch feeds her pups on her own richly nutritious milk – for which, incidentally, cow's milk is a poor substitute – and she also regurgitates food for her growing babies when they beg at her muzzle. The domesticated bitch may indeed follow suit in this rather sick-making ritual, at least until humans take her babies away from her. Puppies grow very rapidly and they need 'little and often' to suit their metabolism and wee stomachs. You may, if you wish, wean a pup on to a 'complete food' soaked in broth or gravy, which gets over all the dietary difficulties in one fell swoop. Otherwise you may choose the more usual varied diet of milk, mince, bread, cereal and biscuits. In either case, pups need four little meals a day. Breakfast and tea should be milk or milk substitute with cereal, and lunch and supper should be pet mince mixed with a little bread or commercial puppy biscuits. You should also ask your vet to examine your puppy to see whether he needs added vitamins A and D or any other supplement to his diet.

As the pup approaches four months, cut out his breakfast and give only three meals, increasing the quantities accordingly. From six to nine months, cut out the other cereal meal, and from nine months onwards, you may give just one good meal if you prefer. Watch the infant's weight and his shape and regulate his diet to keep him plump and bouncy. If he's fat, cut down on the cereal dishes, and if he's thin, bulk up on the cereal and biscuit side, especially if he has diarrhoea. Remember that, if you're feeding a meat-based diet, it should be just that – *not* cereal-based with a spoonful of old scrag-end.

Orphan pups should be kept warm, or they will lapse into a coma. A good pet shop or your own vet should be able to sell you a mother's milk-substitute (such as Welpi) and a puppy-feeding bottle and nozzle or teat. Sterilize the bottle, just as you would for a human baby. When you have fed the pups their lukewarm milk, you will have to massage their little stomachs to help them void their waste, as there is no mother to do this for them. If they are very weak, give them a *little* lukewarm glucose solution every hour by means of a feeding bottle, as well as their milky feeds. Cow's milk is not sufficiently nutritious for pups, so please make sure that you are feeding an approved compound. At three weeks, a tiny pup can be given little feeds of human baby rice (Farlene or Farex) four times a day, and you may gradually add minced meat to this as the pup grows. At eight weeks, puppies are considered fully weaned.

Feeding the pregnant bitch

At about the fourth week of her pregnancy (which lasts nine weeks) the bitch's calcium intake can be increased by giving milk though modern authorities agree that the healthy pregnant bitch should not have her total food intake increased until after whelping. Towards the end of her term, she will need three or four small meals a day because she will feel uncomfortable after large meals. But do consult a good specialist book such as *How to Feed your Dog* by Trevor Turner (Popular Dogs).

Home grooming

Prettiness is not what mongrels are famous for, and you may laugh out loud at pedigree exhibitors frantically brushing their tots where the show judge has disordered them with his hands. But a mongrel who is never groomed or bathed will prove a smelly, flea-ridden, carpet blackening member of your household, and when you take him out for a walk, society will see you reflected in his glory. Matted coats containing parasites lead to skin diseases and bald patches unlikely to put the animal in a good mood, and he may even become surly. Besides, grooming isn't really much trouble if you make it a daily routine, and scientists believe that touching your pet has a good effect on *your* well-being, quite apart from cementing your relationship with the dog.

A puppy should get used to being groomed with a nylon baby's brush from a chemist, to show that it isn't frightening at all. His little face and behind should be wiped with moistened tissues. Stand him on a firm, non-slippery surface that's the right height for you, keeping a hand on him at all times to make sure that he doesn't jump down and hurt himself. As you groom him, examine him for anything unusual. If you do this every day, you'll get to know what is normal in your dog and will notice signs of disease before trouble begins. An adult dog from a shelter should be introduced gradually to his treat – and grooming *is* a treat: dogs will lie on their stomachs waiting to be attended to.

If your orphan is in a very sorry state, he will need to be bathed in lukewarm water, though a dog of uncertain temperament may be quietly sponged down until he gets used to you because bathing may be a bit traumatic. In warm weather you may perform the ablutions in the garden provided that he is kept on a lead and that the lead is securely tied to a fence. You should have all your utensils ready at hand before you start, and enough bowls and buckets ready to shampoo him and rinse the suds out thoroughly as these may irritate his skin.

Start from the back, pouring the water gently. Don't throw a bucketful over him, or he'll have a paroxysm. Tell him what a good dog he is, and don't get any soap in his eyes or ears. A dog shampoo that contains a flea-insecticide – a good one from your vet – will keep him soft, parasite-free and wholesome, though you should follow the makers' instructions carefully, and leave the lather on for as many minutes as they say, or it won't work. Dry him with a couple of old towels and beware of the doggie habits of (a) shaking water all over you and (b) rushing off to look for a good 'stink-roll' to cure his cleanliness.

In cold weather, I'm afraid it's the family tub indoors or, if he's small, a sink. For a large dog, you *can* buy a dry shampoo from the pet shop, which is powdered on and brushed out. Otherwise you may need some assistance in the bathroom. Wear a mac or a bathing costume – you'll need it – and remove from the bathroom anything removable as there will be a lot of splashing about. Use a spray attachment that mixes the water warm and, again, start at the rear end so as not to alarm him. Be quietly determined as you perform this ceremony; most dogs will suffer in silence if they see no escape. Keep your sense of humour, which isn't difficult in the circumstances. Some of the best laughs I've ever had have been during mongrel ablutions.

Towel him down afterwards and then you can use an ordinary hand-held hairdryer, together with your 'grooming utensils' – a nylon prong or stiff bristle brush or a double-sided brush with wire pins one side and nylon tufts the other or, for a short-coated or rough-coated dog, a 'dandy' brush with a strap that goes round your hand. Don't spend a lot of money on grooming equipment. One decent brush and a good non-scratchy metal comb with teeth to suit your dog's coat are really the only essentials, with perhaps a pair of dog toenail clippers and a good supply of tissues, and if you have a potentially shiny dog, you can use an old silk scarf or a shammy leather to 'finish him off'. And that's it. Why pay more?

Stand the dog on a secure surface, then with the dryer in one hand and your brush in the other, rotate your hands as though you were winding bicycle pedals. Brush, dry, brush, dry. You'll find that once you get the knack, this will remove the tangles rhythmically and dry the coat at the same time. If you find a terrible knot, cut it out rather than hurt the dog. No one is going to give your mongrel a fierce scrutinizing in the show ring or count to see that every hair is intact. Once the brushing stage is done, you may find it necessary – and possible – to go through the coat with a comb. Pay careful attention to the dog's face beneath his eyes and around his muzzle, to his feet and where his legs meet his body (his 'armpits'), where treacherous grass seeds may collect, and to his hindquarters, which may need trimming very carefully with a pair of rounded scissors. If you brush and comb your dog each day, you will save yourself a lot of work removing long-established dirt and tangles, and you can also keep an eye out for little black specks of flea dirt on his skin, for which your vet can supply a reliable remedy. How often to bath him? When it's necessary. Some experts claim never to bath their dogs at all because bathing removes the natural oils from the coat and it takes about four days for the coat to normalize. This may be true, but dogs who live a full life roll in ordure and get mucky and smelly, and an occasional bath makes life more pleasant all round.

You can finish your grooming ceremony with a rub-down to bring up any shine your mongrel may possess. A dry coat can

be helped by adding ½–1 teaspoon (2–5 ml) of corn oil to his
dinner. If he's wire-coated, of course, don't bother. If he's
woolly-coated like a poodle, consult a grooming parlour as
he'll almost certainly need clipping if he's to look his best.
Most *other* dogs moult twice a year, in spring and autumn, but
central heating tends to make the moult a chronic condition,
and a good brush and comb on a tiled surface will reduce the
debris on your carpets and furniture, or you can do it outside if
you prefer.

Tar on the feet may be removed with a little medicinal
paraffin and then washed off with soapy water. Large swellings
between the toes may be cysts, needing veterinary attention.
Ears should be examined and the hair inside either plucked
out or combed towards you. Any dirt you see should be
removed very gently with moistened cotton-wool buds. Never
probe a dog's ears – stick to the areas you can see, and if there's
a strange smell or you notice inflammation or a lot of sticky
'canker' (a rather imprecise word for deposits in dogs' ears),
ask the vet, rather than using a 'canker' powder: many of these
contain an insoluble zinc salt that forms a plug and may set up
a distressing infection. If your dog shakes his head a lot or rubs
his head along the ground, suspect ear trouble and phone the
vet.

Eyes should be clear and bright, and swabbed gently to
remove 'sleep'. If you notice tearfulness or discharge, there is
something wrong. Check your pet's teeth for tartar (calculus);
this can be removed by a vet, though you can help prevent it
accumulating by rubbing the teeth with a clean cloth dabbed
in toothpaste or salt. Examine the claws. If they are long and
curved round like a mandarin's, the dog is severely under-
exercised. The only claws that are not worn down naturally are
the dew claws, the dog's thumbnails, which grow round in a
circle and may become embedded in his skin. Dog nail-
clippers of the guillotine kind are easiest to use, but always
leave a quarter of an inch of nail below the quick – a cut dog's
quick is just as painful and bloody as your own, and if you
make a mistake, you will probably not get near his feet
again.

Finally, the area under his tail should be kept clean with

moistened tissues because a long-haired dog with a soiled behind is in considerable discomfort and may squeal with pain when it goes to the lavatory, making you think it is constipated and passers-by think you have ill-treated your dog. If it scrapes its hindquarters along the ground, it may also need to have its anal sacs emptied, as fluid collects in them and causes swelling and inflammation. You can do this yourself wearing rubber gloves and using a thumb and forefinger to squeeze the offending sacs into a tissue – your vet will show you how. You can also help to prevent the impaction of these little glands by ensuring that there is enough roughage in your dog's diet.

Professional grooming

If your dog has a very harsh, long or woolly coat, or if he's big and you fear for your sanity in the bathroom, you should take him to be groomed professionally. These establishments aren't all 'poodle parlours' and the staff don't bite. You can telephone for an appointment at a parlour listed in the Yellow Pages (under 'Dog Grooming') or ask your pet shop for a local address. I went along to East Lodge Grooming, Littlehampton Road, Highdown, Worthing (0903) 506435 and watched the manager Jenny Kearney beautifying some hairy feet shaped like small wellington boots. Jenny is very fond of grooming mongrels because they are so individual. She makes only one rule: no dog, whatever the owner's instructions, should go out looking silly. 'Owners become attached to the tail, or the long ears, or even the eyelashes, and say, "Don't whatever you do touch those!" Not all mongrels need a haircut – Rats and Beanie over there we would simply bath and trim round their feet and ears. My price list covers the more usual breeds, just to give people an idea, and if they have mongrels, they pop in and try to describe the dog to me and I fit it to the nearest type. Really it's priced according to time. Poodly types, because they have to come fairly regularly, get special rates, but none is as expensive as human coiffure.

Some hirsute dogs have a winter scissor-cut and a summer clip, the latter to keep them cool. They look very posh and pleased with themselves. 'Clipping takes the coat a lot shorter. The longest clip is about three-quarters of an inch, whereas if you scissor by hand, you can do any length that the owner requires; it just takes a lot longer. It's nice when it's done. More fluffy. But with mongrels you find that some textures of coat take better to clipping than others. People are inclined to come in with a hairy, shaggy mongrel and say they want it clipped off short, and they expect it to come out looking like a labrador. But it's a different coat, and it comes out slightly woolly, rather than shiny and flat. In hot weather, most owners just say "Take it off – as short as you can." ' Is it wise to have a go yourself? Well, it depends how handy you are, how good the dog is and what type of coat it has. Some people take a pair of scissors to a dog and it looks really awful, and I've seen some home-cut dogs that are not bad jobs at all. But if they want the dog *clipped*, then they had better come to a proper grooming parlour – I don't like the term "poodle parlour" by the way!'

A professional dog-groomer like Jenny can save you literally pounds at the vet's by removing grass seeds before they eat their way into the dog's skin, causing swelling, gunge and big holes like the ravages of some terrible disease. Says Jenny, 'The seeds don't come back out. They just continue forwards.' They are a particular problem for long-haired dogs. What about grooming short-haired ones? 'They moult terribly. Most breeds moult, but poodles, Airedales and other wiry-coated terriers don't really moult and this is why they need clipping. So if you get a mongrel with a predominantly poodle coat – and we have a lot of cross-poodles coming in – they have a woolly coat like a poodle and a long tail, because they weren't docked, and poodles are born with long tails! These dogs have to be clipped the same as a poodle, otherwise their coats just carry on getting longer, woollier and more matted. A haircut cools a dog down, though of course it doesn't in itself prevent moulting – the hair will just be shorter when it comes out. Short-haired dogs should be groomed just as often as long-haired dogs to keep the coat dust-free, clean and shiny, but the actual condition of the coat comes from within. I recommend, for scurfy coats, oil on the dog's dinner. You can buy Vita-pet or just ordinary cod liver oil and lubricate them from the inside out, plus plenty of brushing, and never over-bath a dog.' Frizzy hair? 'They clip quite nicely because they stay woolly and slightly curly. The *most* difficult coats are the type that a border collie has – straight but long. People come in and say they want that trimmed, and it's very difficult; it doesn't work. When it's done you can see the ends, like little lines. So I always advise against trimming those. You usually find that if you trim up the feet, the feathering and under the chest, the dog looks a lot neater anyway.'

How about grooming a mongrel for a show – there are shows for mongrels, after all, such as Scruffts (*see* Chapter 7). 'I'm not really into showing, other than Scruffts!' says Jenny, who happens to be one of the judges at that event. 'If a dog is comfortable, happy and healthy, that suits me fine. I can do without the pompoms and fluffy bits.' The 1984 Scruffts Supreme Champion, Bundle, started scratching on breakfast television and his owner was asked indelicately whether he had fleas. Fleas worry a lot of dog owners. What to do? Jenny recommends Nuvan-Top and Nuvan-Staykill for carpets and bedding. 'I like Vetsyme flea shampoo too, or Shaws double-strength insecticide, followed by Shaws coat dressing as a spray-on conditioner. Some dogs are really allergic to fleas, like my collie. One flea drives him wild and he has to go to the vet's to be given an anti-inflammatory injection.'

What do vets say about the little monsters? I asked Tony Cowie: 'Fleas do not spend all their lives on the host animal. They spend most of their time in your carpets, around central heating pipes, in furniture folds and in the grass outside on a warm day. Then they hop on a warm individual, feed and hop off. So flea control must take account of the environment, denying the flea the chance to feed and breed. Fleas suck the blood of their victims, and there's a tremendous variation in the victim's allergic-type histaminic response; the fat old cat that's sleeping contentedly in the corner may be leaping with fleas, but not sensitive to them. I think the owner should take veterinary advice on an effective compound for fleas because a lot of the cheapies from the pet shop we find do not work. Follow the manufacturer's instructions on frequency of treatments as this is important, and treat the environment as well as the dog – including the fat old cat in the corner!' (It should of course be pointed out that if you have a truly *major* problem, your local council will come and spray your house for you.)

I asked Jenny Kearney about those other important grooming jobs, rear ends and feet. 'Rear ends we do in the bath. A vet told my mother that a dog will scratch behind its ears if its anal glands are impacted, and if I get a dog in that's scratching badly there, I always find that emptying the glands seems to work, even though it's the wrong end of the dog!' But the most sensitive grooming assignments are – *feet*. 'Feet are the worst. Front paws. You get these little fiddly dogs that pull away when you're trying to go in and out of tiny toes with the scissors. They don't care much for toenail-clipping either. Some breeds don't seem to file their claws down naturally themselves and they will grow round and pierce back into the pad, especially dewclaws. So really, apart from being a beauty parlour, we do some things that are quite necessary to the dog's health. Underneath the feet, we take the hair very short so that the dog is walking on clean pads. We do that for every dog, regardless of breed. It prevents them from picking up bubble gum and other nasty things.'

All the dogs I saw in Jenny's parlour – and some come in of their own accord – were very good. What happens when she gets a real rotter of a client that won't behave? 'We do occasionally. We have some muzzles, which we have to use briefly now and then, taking them off as quickly as possible because the dogs don't like them, and we've also got two hooks in the wall for attaching two collars and leads. I don't use holding frames – I don't like them. I think that, if you make a dog that angry and hold it down, you'll do the grooming this time but you'll never get near it again. I think it's mostly fear anyway, and that once they discover you're really not going to hurt them, they're OK. Big dogs that may be a bit reluctant to go in an ordinary bath at home don't mind it here so much because they are in a shallow shower. It's just a question of front feet up, back feet in, and there they are. They're not submerged in water. People tell me, "Oh my dog *hates* water", or "My dog won't stand for the hairdryer", but they react differently in here, I'm pleased to say. I think it's determination as much as anything!'

Teeth and teething

The dog is born toothless and, by five or six weeks, has twenty-eight milk teeth. From four to seven months, these are replaced by a full complement of forty-two permanent choppers for grinding, piercing and shearing (twelve incisors, four canines, sixteen premolars and ten molars), which erupt underneath and push the milk teeth out, usually without problems. During this period though, the youngster longs to chew, as the pegs may irritate him wildly. Please be a bit patient with him during this trying time. Provide a large bone or a cowhide 'chew' bone to give him relief and make a loud noise like a clap of thunder if he chews anything else.

Around six months, there may be a particular phase of mad gnawing that leads to many young mongrels being kicked heartlessly out of doors. Vet Tony Cowie: 'Yes, they're cutting their back teeth. The front teeth come through from four-and-a-half months onwards. I think it's a behaviour syndrome akin to teething in babies howling at night and wetting the bed. Whether dogs chew because their mouths hurt or just to exercise their teeth, a dirty great big raw marrow bone will be chewed in preference to the furniture. On the other hand, puppies do tend to gnaw because they're bored with being shut in. They need scolding, but they also need exercise. There are repellent sprays that you can try, but I don't personally find them very effective.'

Sloppy diets are bad for doggie dentures and although a dog's teeth do not usually suffer from caries like decaying human teeth, they do accumulate tartar that can cause gum disease and loosening fangs. Try to ensure that there's something crunchy in your dog's diet and clean his teeth with a cloth or even a toothbrush. Occasionally during teething, canine teeth coming through can cause a youngster problems if the milk teeth do not eject naturally. In this case your vet can remove them under anaesthetic.

Ailments

If you notice anything unusual when grooming your dog, or if he is lethargic, irritable or off his food, there may be something wrong. Wet noses are not the best guide to a dog's health; a sleep near the fire will cause a dry nose whereas some diseases do not. A better guide is the dog's appetite, excessive thirst, discharge, vomiting, diarrhoea or general listlessness. If you put your coat on to take him out and he can't be bothered, the poor old devil may be ill. Take his temperature rectally using a snub-nosed glass thermometer from the chemist's, shaken down and smeared with Vaseline. (After you've read it, shake it again and wipe it clean with cotton-wool soaked in surgical spirit.) The thermometer should be inserted about an inch (2.5 cm) into the rectum and held there for half a minute, and if necessary you should have someone else on hand to hold the dog's head and keep him very still and quiet.

A healthy dog's temperature ranges between 101.0° and 101.6°F (38.3–38.7°C), although excitement may force this up to 101.8°F (38.8°C) and even 102.0°F (39°C). Anything outside this range indicates a problem. Telephone your vet immediately for an appointment. And please do consult a vet. Don't rely on your own diagnostic powers unless you are very experienced. A dog cannot talk or tell you its symptoms and the wrong medicine is worse than none at all. A very good piece of advice comes from a vet, R. C. G. Hancock, who says never treat an illness you cannot diagnose and never treat anything for long. If the symptoms don't clear up after two or three days, ask for help. Vets spend a good deal of their time treating dogs for syndromes brought about by incorrect home remedies, and giving your dog an aspirin may mask signs that are the veterinarian's guide to disease. Please do not bodge. Ask for advice; a phone call costs less than a potion.

Mongrels are stout-hearted creatures and will often shake off minor ailments on their own by sleeping up in some dark corner. But be observant. Look for signs of pain and lameness, abnormal breathing or delirium. And if the vet tells you on the phone to bring the dog to the surgery, do keep him on his lead – all the time. Vets do not appreciate frantic pets racing round

Aborigines with their dingoes

Earliest 'breeds' would be inadmissable to Crufts

THE TURNSPIT

THE BAN-DOG

THE BULL-DOG

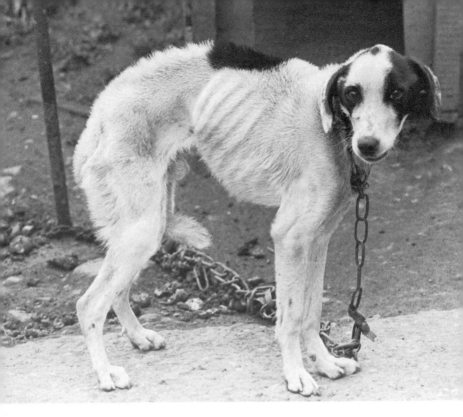

The Great Escape – RSPCA pups bid for freedom

Bones before *(left)* and after *(above)* – the work of the RSPCA in restoring the unwanted. It took six weeks to transform Bones from this emaciated wreck to a healthy dog. When found chained in a packing case he could hardly stand

Morning rounds – the Battersea van making another delivery

Jason modelling the Japanese anti-bark collar (batteries removed!)

Not an animal National Health Service, the PDSA do a sterling job for owners who genuinely cannot afford vets' fees

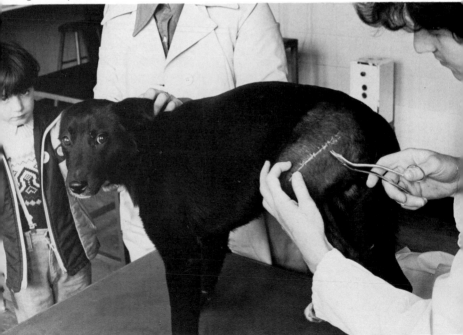

their consulting rooms and biting their behinds. Describe the symptoms as accurately as you can, and write them down if necessary. You'd be surprised how many owners get to the surgery and forget what was worrying them. Even in an emergency, always try to telephone *before* you arrive, for a booking. This may save you and your sick pet a wasted journey.

Health directory

ACCIDENTS If your dog is involved in an accident, don't panic but get him to the vet's as quickly as possible, even if you have to call a cab or thumb a lift. If the dog is unconscious, slide a blanket or a piece of hardboard under him and lift him into the car stretcher-wise – he may have internal injuries. Keep him warm. A dog is not dead if you can feel a pulse inside its thigh. Flick the animal's tongue forward and rest its head on one side. It is possible to give heart massage, artificial respiration and even the kiss of life to a dog, just as to a human.

BANDAGE MUZZLE If a dog is liable to bite, through pain or fear, you must improvise a soft muzzle with a length of bandage or an old nylon stocking or tie. Tie it in a firm half-knot under the dog's lower jaw, cross over the ends and tie them behind his ears in a fairly tight bow. The muscles for opening his jaws are not as strong as the ones for closing them so you don't have to wire his teeth together or anything like that. This simple soft muzzle will enable you to handle a sick or injured dog without being snapped at.

BLEEDING Arrest bleeding by direct pressure over the wound, using a sterile cold compress. If blood seeps through this, add more dressings on *top* of the first; don't remove it. If the wound is to a limb, you may apply a tourniquet by means of a bandage a few inches from the wound that is tightened with a pencil twisted round like a propeller, but *never* leave a tourniquet on for more than ten minutes or you may damage tissue. If the blood is bright red and spurting, the damage is to an artery. Arterial wounds require the tourniquet *above* the bleeding. If the blood is dark red, it comes from a vein. Venous wounds require the tourniquet *below* the bleeding. In serious wounds, the bleeding may be from both veins and arteries. In this case, you must apply a cold compress, hold tight and send for help.

CANINE PARVOVIRUS, HARDPAD AND DISTEMPER, HEPATITIS, LEPTOSPIROSIS Avoidable killers. Your dog should be protected by vaccination before they strike. Please don't wait around for symptoms; it may be too late.

COUGHING This may be due either to obstruction (see below) or infection of the windpipe or lungs. In either case you should consult a vet, unless you can see the offending obstruction and remove it yourself. Kennel cough, so-called because of its prevalence in kennels, reaches epidemic proportions in summertime and its chief symptom is a harsh, nagging cough that may end in frothing, with the dog bowing its head towards the ground as though trying to expel something from its throat. Treatment is by antibiotics prescribed by the vet, but you may give the dog a linctus cough mixture or a couple of teaspoons of honey to soothe his tubes. Kennel cough may last several weeks or clear up in a few days, so unless the dog is otherwise run-down, don't worry unduly. There is a vaccine now available for dogs likely to be exposed to infection.

DOG BITES If your mongrel is bitten by another dog, seek veterinary advice, especially if the wound is a puncture, although it does not bleed profusely. Otherwise it may become infected. Staunch bleeding as above.

EAR MITES These tiny hairy grey charmers live in the ear canal and surrounding tissue and are transferable from cats to dogs. They cause a collection of dark waxy stuff in the ear that looks like brown sugar, and may lead to more serious problems if untreated. Your vet will prescribe an insecticide that may have to be repeated at intervals and also be administered to any cats you may have.

FIRST-AID   Why not keep a first-aid kit for your dog? Accidents are *always* unexpected and a little sponge-bag containing your mongrel's bits and pieces will be a great comfort and help in times of panic. You will need some crêpe bandages, sticking plasters, a plastic syringe without a needle (for squirting medicine), gauze, scissors, cotton-wool, a thermometer and some disinfectant suitable for animal use such as Tego or Savlon – always read the instructions carefully.

FITS   Remove anything from the room that the dog may knock over and put a guard round the fire. Leave the dog alone, other than to remove his collar. Convulsions are usually preceded and followed by a confused daze, during which your pet may not know who you are. Keep him quiet and warm and consult the vet as soon as possible. Fits *may* be caused by poisoning. Look around for anything dubious the dog may have sampled.

FRACTURES   Seek veterinary help immediately and beware of even a mild-mannered dog snapping from the pain. If necessary, apply a soft muzzle as directed above. Lift the dog into a car by means of a blanket hammock and be sure that his weight is not resting on the injury.

GIVING LIQUID MEDICINE   Tell your dog to sit and then bend down at his side. Gently grasp his muzzle with one hand to keep his mouth closed (this is not difficult), and with the other hand, make a little pouch of his lips where his upper and lower jaws join. If you put your index finger in the fold, you'll find it pops out naturally in a little 'bag' at the side of his mouth, so don't tell me you can't find it. Then all you do is to tilt the dog's head up and pour the offending medicine into his pouch, relaxing your hold on his jaws sufficiently to allow him to swallow. If you really can't manage this using a spoon, you can drip the liquid down by means of a plastic needleless syringe. Stop if he coughs and splutters. Praise the dog for being so good, even if he hasn't been.

GIVING PILLS For this one, you need the dog's mouth open, obviously. Have a titbit ready – something he really likes. Grasp his upper jaw by pressing his lips gently into his mouth behind his canine fangs with your thumb and forefinger. (There are two little gaps there for the purpose. Be especially careful if there is a small tooth in the gap.) Hold the pill in your free hand, poised, and with the middle finger of that hand pull the dog's lower jaw down. This will also give your hand something to rest on. Then you just place the pill on the base of his tongue, as far back as you can push it, withdraw your hand and hold the jaws shut gently. Stroke his throat gently. If he doesn't swallow naturally, this is where the titbit comes in. Hold it near his nose. That will make his mouth water and he'll be obliged to swallow. Then just give him the titbit. This method is more effective than trying to conceal pills in the dog's food: canines are very crafty and can detect bad grits at twenty paces. He'll probably eat the food and spit the pills on the floor.

HEART ATTACK Although the symptoms of heart attack are sometimes mistaken for a fit (see above), the owner will usually have been alerted to the former by earlier signs of a heart condition and will realize what is happening. Severe difficulty in breathing, a low-pitched, deep coughing in the morning or at night, inability to exercise and bluish-coloured gums or tongue are all signs of heart disease. Call the vet at once, lie the dog on its right side, and if the tongue and gums are already turning blue, give the dog heart massage by pushing rhythmically against the chest. The chance of cardiac arrest is higher in elderly dogs, as in elderly humans, and a fat dog is particularly at risk.

HEATSTROKE Symptoms are: panting, increased pulse rate, vomiting, congested mucous membranes, and a worried expression. If unrelieved, heatstroke is likely to lead to coma and death. Put the dog in a draught and apply cold water to his head and coat. If the animal is prostrate and losing consciousness, call the vet immediately. Never, ever leave your mongrel locked in a car in the summer sun. Park in the shade, leave the window open a few inches for air, and check periodically to see that the dog is all right.

HOMOEOPATHY   In recent years, concern about the use of drugs and animal suffering in vivisection laboratories has led many people to turn as patients to alternative medicine. Although cranks have always abounded in the field of canine care, and quacks should never be trusted with your dog's health, there is one branch of alternative medicine that has a respectable and scientifically validated record in animal treatment – homoeopathy. The principle of homoeopathic medicine is that it treats 'like with like', that is to say, it treats symptoms with tiny dilutions of substances that would actually cause those symptoms in a healthy organism. Homoeopathy is favoured by the Royal Family and describes itself not as an alternative but *the* alternative to conventional medicine (which homoeopaths call 'allopathy'). The best book I have seen on the subject of animal treatment is by a vet, George MacLeod MRCVS DVSM – *The Homoeopathic Treatment of Dogs*, published by the Homoeopathic Development Foundation – or you can telephone Ainsworths Homoeopathic Pharmacy in London to ask about other titles (*see* Appendix 6 for addresses and telephone numbers). If you are worried about drugs or vivisection, I believe you will find the literature most interesting.

JAUNDICE   If your mongrel appears 'liverish', i.e. the whites of his eyes or his lips and gums have a sallow, yellowish tinge, suspect trouble. Liver inflammation may be due to infection or even poisoning and the sooner he gets treatment the better. Do not neglect the symptoms of liver dysfunction – they may be very serious.

LAMENESS   Limping may be due to a split pad or tar, chewing gum or a grass seed in the paw, but lameness for which there is no obvious cause should always be referred to a vet. Arthritis (inflammation of the joints) is not uncommon in elderly dogs.

LUMPS Tumours range from benign swellings and cysts to malignant cancers. On bitches it is always advisable to check each mammary gland now and then for lumps and bumps. Elderly dogs tend to suffer from benign wart-like tumours of the sebaceous glands, which resemble little cauliflowers. These are generally quite harmless, but *all* such lumps should be seen by a vet.

NEPHRITIS Inflammation of the kidneys. Frequent urination and unusual thirst, especially if accompanied by vomiting or weight loss, should be reported to the vet. A dog with a kidney infection may walk with a 'hunched up' posture because of the pain. Leptospirosis, which may attack the kidneys, is a killer disease for which your dog should have been inoculated. If you are reading this and he hasn't, please see to it straightaway. Inoculations usually combine the kidney injections with distemper etc. Annual boosters are required.

OBSTRUCTIONS IN THE MOUTH A piece of bone or stick lodged in the roof of the dog's mouth may only be removed by working it backwards, where the teeth are further apart. If you pull forwards you are jamming it tighter. Hold the dog's head in such a way that the dislodged object doesn't fall down the animal's throat. Don't panic. A police dog section commander friend of mine got a tennis ball out of a German Shepherd's throat after it lost consciousness, though it is not advisable to wait till then. A vet can certainly remove the object under anaesthetic. The main thing is for you to keep calm, or you will frighten the dog further.

POISONING If you suspect the dog has swallowed a corrosive substance (e.g. bleach), leave him alone and call the vet immediately. If the substance is non-corrosive, then you should make the dog sick by giving him a couple of little lumps of washing soda, using the method for giving pills (see above). If you haven't got any soda, use salt water. Then take him posthaste to the veterinary surgery.

SCALDS AND BURNS   Try not to contaminate the wound – it is sterile at the moment. Apply cold water from the tap and a sterile gauze dressing and if there is extensive damage, take the dog to the vet. If the wound is small, you may be able to clip away the hair before applying the gauze. For acid burns, you should apply a solution of sodium bicarbonate. For alkali burns, use a vinegar solution. Always tell the vet what you've done before he examines the wound, so as not to mislead him.

SCRATCHING   Parasites of the dog are unfortunately not limited to the flea. Dogs also occasionally pick up lice, ticks, mange, mites and ringworm. Part the fur at the site of the irritation to see what you're dealing with. Nuvan Top aerosol is effective against fleas, lice, ticks, some form of mange and other ectoparasites (i.e. those on the skin) and can be obtained from the vet, but do *not* use it on a dog that has been wearing a flea-collar or on sore or inflamed areas. If you see lesions on the skin, whether self-inflicted or not, take your itchy dog to the vet because it may have eczema or an allergy. Whatever remedy you use, follow the maker's instructions.

SNEEZING   Apply cotton-wool soaked in cold water or ice in a clean handkerchief to the bridge of the dog's nose. Sneezing may be due to a bit of grass or an insect in his nostril, which will have to be removed, either by yourself or professionally.

SPAYING   Ovario-hysterectomy (removal of womb and ovaries). Widely recommended by vets for a non-breeding bitch not only for birth control but for her own well-being. Veterinary surgeon Tony Cowie: 'There is a balance of pros and cons, and the balance on the pro side is basically the birth control problem, the unwanted puppies problem, the convenience of not having seasons – which is six weeks a year in a bitch's life when it has to be kept fairly well isolated – and the very real problem that the alternative to all this is messing around with chemical controls. There are, as you know, injections and pills, and I think the veterinary profession is happy to use them once in a blue moon, but certainly these treatments are not to be used *ad nauseam* throughout a bitch's life.

'There is clinical evidence that if you chemically inhibit a very active system over a long period, you end up with some sort of "ladies' problem" later on – womb troubles, pyometras [potentially fatal uterine infections], mammary cancers, that sort of thing. Now, these will also occur in a bitch that is not *allowed* to breed; we find incidence of such problems in bitches that have been kept in during their seasons – mammary tumours, for example, quite a lot of maiden bitches do tend to get these, yet they don't occur nearly so much in bitches that have been spayed. So you've got convenience, you've got birth control, and you've got what I personally believe is a prolongation of the bitch's life. I find that, statistically, spayed bitches live longer and are happier, and I would shout that from the treetops. Now, having said that, somebody will undoubtedly jump up and say, "Well, I've never had my bitches spayed, and I've never had any trouble at all." '

Jane Lilley, Assistant Editor of *Dogs Monthly*: 'I consider the RSPCA's policy *recommending* spaying quite misleading. Spaying is a *major* operation and, if you like, mutilation. There was and still is an outcry about such comparatively minor surgery as docking or removal of dewclaws while cropping of ears is now forbidden in this country. Nowhere do the RSPCA point out the side-effects that can occur following spaying or castration, nor do they detail just how carefully a bitch must be watched, confined and not allowed to leap or climb for at least ten days until her stitches are removed. I would never sell any of my puppies to people intending to have them spayed.'

Tony Cowie: 'Well of course, on the other side of the argument, you *do* have the fact that you're putting them through a major abdominal routine and, to vets, it *is* routine, although you do have the small but very real risk associated with anaesthesia. The incidence of mortality is *very* low. You *are* interfering with a major department within the body, the female reproduction department, and yes, there are problems associated with that, such as possible obesity in bitches that have been spayed. Quite a lot of bitches don't need their previous intake of food because a very active system has been removed and their energy requirements may be less. We advise our clients to cut down by about 15 per cent if the bitch starts to put on weight. But not many bitches have this problem. The other difficulty that you can have is urinary incontinence, the so-called "dribbling-syndrome". Again, statistically very low, and it can be controlled with a very low-dosage hormone replacement, usually in the form of a tablet, perhaps once or twice a week.

'Now, I throw all those pros and cons into the washing machine and each time come out with the advisability of having a bitch spayed, unless of course you want to breed from her. I have had five bitches and mine have all been spayed. My current rescue dog decided to have a pyometra a week before we went on holiday: she was only two. In this case, the spaying was a life-saving operation because there's no way she would have got better. Spaying is simple, it's routine, it's everyday. Let them have a season, because we find that the problems of spaying are very much reduced by allowing the bitch to reach full sexual maturity before she is spayed, and have her done between her first and second seasons.'

UTERINE INFECTIONS   Unspayed bitches often suffer from infections of the uterus. Any discharge that occurs between seasons should be investigated by a vet.

VOMITING AND DIARRHOEA   This may be due to a variety of causes. A change of diet may upset a dog's stomach, not through any fault of the food itself, but because the animal's system is slow to adjust. Vomiting just once is usually no cause for concern, as dogs make themselves sick with grass quite deliberately, but frequent vomiting, especially if accompanied by diarrhoea, may indicate something more serious. If the dog appears listless or irritable, don't delay seeking advice.

WORMS   Puppies should be routinely wormed for round-worms on a monthly basis until 6–7 months old. Adult dogs should be dosed perhaps two or three times a year. Tapeworms require treatment if evident. (*See* chapter 2.)

Piperazine preparations are effective against roundworms and also broad spectrum 'complete wormers' available from vets, which cover both roundworms and tapeworms.

6
Mongrel behaviour

People who look down on dogs are quite misguided. The dog is far more 'sensible' than we are. During my research for *Your Obedient Servant*, I met drug-detection dogs who could find contraband at thirty yards, wrapped in four plastic bags and suspended in a tank of coolant fluid. I was introduced to mine-detection dogs (the Army do not care for the expression 'sniffers') who could pathfind more accurately than the latest anomaly detectors and locate plastic as easily as metal. When a veterinary scientist removed test dogs' scenting membranes as an experiment, they could still find their mines. I met police dogs who could trace a coin in a field or a man in a factory full of people in the twinkling of an eye, and who could give their handlers a picture of what happened at the scene of a crime several hours before. I found out how bloodhounds located Martin Luther King's assassin, James Earl Ray, in the hills of East Tennessee and how wartime messengers, conscripted from the dogs' homes, worked infallibly in the dark through heavy bombardment over terrain they had never seen before. I discovered how a dog found its way from Hammersmith to a trench in Armentières to rejoin his master; how a police dog in a haunted house, fearless as it was against the gun and the stick, refused to enter the room where the sighting of the ghost occurred; how dogs have given warnings of deaths and earthquakes; and how another police dog, Queenie, tried to tell her handler that the Harrods bomb was about to go off. Scientists have their theories, but frankly they are baffled by these canine abilities. Perhaps your mongrel, lying on the living-room carpet, has knowledge that spans this universe, but in any case it is certainly worth your while trying to understand his behaviour. You may learn something to your advantage.

Senses

Dogs are not colour blind, as was once believed, but the balance of rod-receptors to cones in the retinas of their eyes is tuned more finely for movement rather than stationary objects, for dim light rather than bright light. A shepherd can wave his hand to his dog a mile away and the dog will see it, though it may miss a cat sitting stock still just a few yards off. This is probably because the animal, as well as being more sensitive to movement, also switches to scent rather than sight to locate prey close at hand. Dogs are more sensitive to lower light levels and can see better in the dark than we can. Pups in the wild are born underground, and feral dogs in hot countries have been observed to be nocturnal.[1] Each of a dog's eyes has a tapetum, or reflector, for intensifying light signals, which shines yellow in the dark. Their field of vision is wider than a man's, 180°–270° (according to the animal's head shape), because the dog's eyes are situated towards the sides of his face. But he has less binocular (double-eyed) vision than man, and therefore less depth perception. Some authorities suggest that a dog actually has 'second sight' – and that he can perceive an 'aura' of events that have already taken place beyond the range of man's visual perception, rather like a medium.

A dog's sense of smell may be at least one hundred times better than ours. The layered scenting membranes in his nose may cover 130 sq. cm, compared with 3 sq. cm of adult human membranes, and there are forty times more cells in his brain for dealing with scent information than the human equivalent. A wet nose helps the canine to smell by dissolving scent molecules in the air and bringing them into contact with his proboscis. He also has a pair of apertures in the roof of his mouth with which he 'tastes' the air for clues (*Flehmen*).

A dog's hearing outclasses man's, registering ultrasonic frequencies up to 35 kilohertz compared with our range of up to 20 kilohertz. A dog can also detect sound at four times the distance picked up by man, and immediately recognize the difference between true C and C sharp and between two metronomes clicking at 96 and 100 beats per minute.[2] He is extremely sensitive to vibrations, and some scientists think he can detect minute thermal differences with a heat sensor in his nose, rather like infra-red photographic equipment.

He can tell the time fairly accurately, and one American scientist believes that dogs can navigate by a combination of an internal clock and the angle of the sun, bringing the two into alignment to ensure that they find themselves in the right place at the right time, like migrating birds. Professor Michael Fox thinks that this is how individual dogs have travelled mighty distances to rejoin their owners, switching over to scent and sight clues once they got within range. And stories of the dog's 'telepathic' and 'psychic' abilities are numerous (*see* Chapter 12).

Signs

Dogs communicate with one another by means of highly complex canine Esperanto, or 'Chumfo' (as it has been called), of signs, signals, stares, stances, scents and sounds that include a whole range of grunts, growls, whines, yelps, barks and howls. Humans who take the trouble to find out the rudiments of this language are privy to special knowledge of canine customs, which will save them the heartbreak of trying to stamp out habits engrained in dogs for thousands of years.

For example, dogs anoint their faeces with chemical traces from their anal sacs, identifiable by other dogs who sniff and occasionally eat the sacred pile (coprophagia). This is thought to provide B vitamins, seed their stomachs with local micro-organisms and intensify the scent information left by the previous owner. The habit of rolling in carrion and ordure is believed to have a different origin, to do with the dog disguising its scent for hunting work, looking big in the pack, and absorbing certain fatty acids to enhance its sense of smell. Dogs will also scratch earth and leaves over their own urine and droppings, either to conceal them or to mark the ground with secretions from interdigital scent glands on their feet. The other great chemical messenger, urine, contains decodable traces that impart information about the dog's identity, his sex, his territory and when he was last in the vicinity. This is why dogs are always 'marking' walls and lamp-posts – it has nothing to do with lavatorial functions. Male dogs may mark indoors to advertise their sexual prowess in the locality and 'sign' what they consider to be their territory.

To understand all may not be to forgive all, but it helps. Vet Tony Cowie: 'They do it because they like your house and they're proud of it. Look at the dog in the wild – you'll see it going round its territory peeing in every corner saying this is my domain. There's one type of marking though that we often see in the surgery, where the dog has perhaps got a urinary problem – say, a stone in his bladder – and he feels uncomfortable, and in this case I think he may be trying to tell you something. But the actual behavioural problem is related to dogs that perhaps feel threatened by signs or smells outside and they want to exert their influence within the room. There are hormonal treatments that you can try to stop it, but sometimes these have a nil response. It's the sort of problem that a vet would refer to an animal psychologist like Roger Mugford when clinically there's nothing wrong, and I've had 100 per cent success with my referrals to him. Of course, dogs do mark, too, in the presence of bitches. If there's a bitch in season in the area, the old dog thinks, aye aye, I'll go round putting my aftershave and pheremones on things all over the place, which is supposed to have a subliminal effect.'

Because dogs, like wolves, are, at least potentially, pack animals, they are in a very high league of social communication; they have to be, in order to survive. Signals go out concerning prey, territory, mates, status and kinship as well as declarations of war, just as they do between humans. Indeed, dog relationships may be quite as complicated as our own, even if they are not actually on speaking terms. Dogs are adept at reading our body language because they use it themselves. A trainee may get confused by the command 'Forward' if the handler suddenly leads off with his left foot instead of his right, and dogs are aware of tiny physical signals that mean 'He's going to get my lead now' and 'He's coming home because she's taken his plate out of the cupboard.' Your mongrel may well ignore your shouting at him, and yet immediately hide under the table when he sees your 'genuinely angry' posture, or detects a slight change in the register of your voice.

The body language of dogs has been studied by scientists since Charles Darwin. Most readers will be familiar with the 'play bow' of a sportive dog, with his 'elbows' resting on the ground and his backside in the air, tail waving. Teasing with a toy is another canine invitation to play. Then there's the wag, a sign of arousal. Unfortunately this has led to occasional misunderstandings between dogs and their owners who have mistaken their angry charge's thrashing member for an indication of pleasure. Smiling, on the other hand, is not so much a snarl as a gesture of appeasement, especially if accompanied by other signs of supplication such as laid-back ears and lowly crouching. As dogs do not show cheesecake grins to one another, it seems they may have learned the habit from their observations of humans. The licking of faces is a sign of great trust and need between a puppy and his dam, and muzzle-grasping, translated in the human sphere as nose-grasping, is a friendly greeting to a superior member of the pack. Other greetings include galloping runs and leaps, whines, wags and frenzied bouncing, of which an adopted mongrel may not know the decorous limits.

Then there are the 'fighting' and 'peace' signals. A dominant confident dog will 'look big' by stalking, raising his head, tail, ears, hackles and guard hairs. His inferior will be made to 'feel small', tucking his tail under, bowing his head, crouching down and even lying on his back on the ground to show his little pink tummy. His ears will be back and his eyes narrowed in supplication as if to say, 'Don't waste your teeth on humble me, your Highness.' A dog will behave submissively like this over a misdeed for which you have corrected him, not because of any sense of 'guilt' but because he detects the threatening anger in your behaviour. (All dogs are, in fact, not guilty, so far as they themselves are concerned.) There are also combinations of these gestures. A dog that is signalling aggression through fear may lay back his ears *and* raise his hackles. He may crouch down and draw back the sides of his mouth to expose the buccal cavities at the sides of his teeth (signs of fear) and yet he may also bite.

The greatest danger of a fight comes when the status of two dogs is in dispute, just as with many human males. The fine balance may be upset by injury, or ageing, or somebody misguidedly tugging on the dog's lead, making him appear weak and foolish. Under these circumstances the adversary will often seize the main chance, and anything else he can get his fangs into. The best anti-fight weapon is not lead-tugging or plaintive accusation, but water, if available, thrown liberally over *both* combatants. Don't try to wade into the mêlée – you'll only get hurt, because in such a crisis your dog doesn't know you from Erwin Rommel. Dogs that have already 'settled their hash' will often avoid looking at one another, as interdog staring usually betokens trouble. Apart from territorial considerations, there is also believed to be a recognized fight distance between two potential combatants that, if it is invaded, signals the end of the peace treaty. An intervening fence between the foes may shorten this distance considerably and cause a flare-up. On the other hand, a dog barking at you through the fence will not necessarily attack you through the gate.

All dogs, bitches included, will 'mark' on their walks, and there is a courtship dance and much ceremony between two amorous dogs, which usually begins with furious wagging and nose-nuzzling, proceeds through various stages of passion in which the male dog rests his chin on the female's back, and ends with mating and a 'tie' – the curious canine rump-to-rump stance that may last for up to an hour, during which the pair are literally inseparable. This is quite normal and natural, and attempts to separate them by force may wound the dogs in very sensitive places. Mongrels are ardent lovers, and a dog who senses a neighbourhood bitch on heat will fight to beat a path to her door, ignoring food and drink, and camping outside for days, following anyone who comes out bearing her fragrance. Frustrated, he will mount cushions and grandmother's legs in the house, unless his testosterone secretion is shut down artificially by a vet.

Dogs out hunting have a repertoire of pursue-and-kill behaviour, including tremendous gazelle-like leaps into the undergrowth and a steady stalk, with the head and body held still and the legs hurrying violently in the direction of the intended victim. A dog about to sleep will circle round and round in a sort of grass-crushing ceremony, redolent of primeval forests. Watching these strange rituals of *Canis familiaris* is not only entertaining: it transports the owner to another world, a Paradise Regained where intellect and words are irrelevant. Some scientists have been so intrigued by Chumfo and doggie rites that they have spent their lives following feral dogs in such diverse places as America, Madras and Mexico, minutely observing their behaviour. One such researcher is Professor Michael Fox, here studying the aforementioned trio in St Louis, Missouri (*see* p.2):

> 3.55 a.m.: Trio sleeping. F [female] stands up, looks at Y. Y immediately sits up. F gets off patio and goes on to sidewalk and looks back at X and Y. She then sets off down the road. Y stands up. F stops and looks back at Y. Y now follows her. X still sleeps. Y looks back at X, then follows F. After 5 min, Y and F return to patio. F tail-wags at X who is still sleeping. Y sits close by and tail-wags. X sits up. Y moves off. F waits by X. Y returns to porch and tail-wags at F. F goes on to sidewalk and looks back at X. X stands up, marks twice and Y marks and scrapes. Y crosses road and looks back at F. F (in middle of the road) looks back at X, who joins her 'at last'. She gives a tail-wag, face bump and exaggerated head turn to X and then leads him across the road to join up with Y. With F in the lead, Y and X follow her to forage.[3]

Sexuality

Domestic dogs are much more promiscuous than their wild relations, perhaps by reason of human interference in their affairs. Most domesticated bitches have two heats, or oestrus periods, a year (compared with the she-wolf's solitary heat around February). The bitch is usually sexually mature by eight to twelve months, earlier than her wild relatives, and her heats last from eighteen to twenty-one days, though she will only allow a dog to mate with her at the height of this season.

Heat is characterized by swelling of the vulva and by bleeding, which most bitches will clean up themselves. The animal is shedding the lining of her womb, and during this early period of about ten days, she is highly attractive to male dogs of her realm, and will announce her coming out by passing drops of urine on her walks if you exercise her in the streets during her publicity drive. You can buy deodorants to mask her scent, or oil of citronella, but you must spray your door and gateposts as well as the bitch's bottom. Between the tenth and fourteenth days of her heat, she reaches peak acceptance, during which she will stand to be served by what she considers a decent suitor, holding her tail aside. From the fourteenth day onwards, her interest is starting to flag, and by day 21 the oestrus is usually over.

If she has been mated she will bear her pups after the nine-week gestation common to dogs. If not she may well suffer a pseudo (false) pregnancy, triggered by the hormone progesterone in her body. She may lose her appetite, vomit, cuddle a lump of wood or a precious toy, make various 'nests' with old rags or paper, dig furiously in the garden to make a burrow, and become tetchy with humans of the household who always behave unreasonably towards a poor girl at this difficult time. She can't help it. She will even produce milk for her phantom pups. The cure for her condition is not to 'let her have a litter'. This will not prevent her from having false pregnancies in the future, nor will it take the edge off her maternal instincts. The cure for her ills is spaying, which is safe, permanent and fairer to her than chemicals such as the canine contraceptive pill, prescribed all her life (bitches do not have a menopause), or imprisonment for three weeks twice a year. Spaying will not turn her into a brainless fat frump. All Guide Dogs and many police bitches are neutered.

If an unspayed bitch accidentally gets out during her season and is mated, or if a neighbourhood male breaks into your garden or scales your six-foot fence (these things do happen), pregnancy may be averted within thirty-six hours by an injection, though this will prolong her heat for the next three weeks. Such injections are purely for emergencies and may have side-effects if administered incautiously. Unless you want a lot of mongrel pups and *can find them homes*, please consider neutering the norm. To have strong maternal instincts with no possibility of fulfilment must be the unkindest cut of all.

Anyone reading Jilly Cooper's book, *Intelligent and Loyal*, will know how hot-blooded and pugnacious male mongrels can be in pursuit of a finely turned paw. One of the main motives for the mongrel problem of wandering is to look for bitches on heat. You may like to think of the male mongrel going forth and propagating his kind, but since hundreds of thousands of strays are put down every year, there would seem to be more than enough of his kind already. There are three answers to male mongrel sexuality: letting him out, keeping him in or having him either chemically or surgically castrated. The first is inexcusable, the second frustrating and the third clinical, achieved by the injection of female hormones or removal of the testicles. Vasectomy, though it is possible in dogs, does not generally alter the dog's sexual desires, nor the aggression or wanderlust associated with them. Neither, it must be said, does letting him mate – in fact, the latter may make him ten times worse. I'm a great standard-bearer for mongrel rights and will challenge anyone to a duel who says they haven't got any, but until we get the problem of unwanted and homeless mongrels sorted out, I believe we have a responsibility to keep down the population as best we can. Castration, the surgical removal of the testes, seems to be a less common procedure than spaying. Some vets will decline to perform the operation. Both castration and vasectomy will prevent the male impregnating the female, though sadly there is no *guarantee* that even castration will abolish desire. A few neutered males continue as randy as before! If you *do* decide to mate your pet, then do what proud owners such as Jilly Cooper have done and find him or her a partner whose owners will be as pleased about the puppies as yourselves. That is, if the dogs *like* each other. I'm not recommending clone marriages and forced matings such as those that take place in the pedigree world – heaven forbid that mongrels should be reduced to that!

The pregnant bitch
Ensure that she has been wormed and is generally in good

health and that inoculations are up to date. Notify your vet in advance of the happy day; in the very unlikely event of your needing to call him out, he will appreciate the courtesy of a warning. (If you're not sure she is pregnant, an X-ray at six weeks will confirm it, but better avoided if possible.) Give her her regular exercise until the latter stages of her pregnancy, when she will prefer to cut down. The pups are in their own little water-bag to protect them from bumps, so there's no need to carry her about in a sedan chair. Prepare for the birth by providing the bitch with a nice big cardboard box with an entrance cut out of the side. This will be her nesting box, and should replace her own bed towards the great day. Give her lots of newspaper; she will probably like to tear it up herself for her bedding. If you give any blanket, it should be a cellular one that will not suffocate her babies. Put the whelping box in a warm secluded place: she may choose a spot herself where you could accommodate her, if not too inconvenient.

For the birth itself, you will need very little. Miscarriages are rare in mongrels, and most mongrel bitches make excellent and competent mothers. All that she asks is warmth, her food and milk, an old box and a bit of privacy. Please don't make an exhibition of her or she may delay the birth and neglect her babies. Be near her, praise her, but try not to interfere at all if you can possibly help it.

As the birth approaches, she will begin to pant, change her bed around and wander in ever-decreasing circles, and when labour begins, after perhaps a day and night of this behaviour, she will start to strain. The appearance of a grey balloon at the vulva signals the imminent arrival of pup number one, who should make his debut about half an hour after straining sets in (if he takes more than two hours, there may be something wrong – call the vet). The bitch will break the grey water bag by licking and will bite through the umbilical cord, and she will also remove the protective membrane from the puppy, to enable it to breathe. In the *unlikely* event of her neglecting to do this, you should first ensure that the bitch has severed the umbilical cord. If not, snap it yourself with your fingers, leaving an inch or two attached to the baby – this will quickly disappear. If you are squeamish and have to use scissors, run them under boiling water beforehand to sterilize them, and let them cool down. Bleeding is normal. Then you should clear the pup's airways by wiping his little face with a clean towel and rubbing his head gently. If he isn't breathing, support his head and swing him between your knees to force air into his lungs. Many emergencies of this sort respond to the Big Dipper. A dark green discharge accompanies doggie births, and ten or so minutes later comes the afterbirth, which the bitch will eat (it contains nutrients).

An average mongrel litter is four to eight plump pups, all rather individual; the record confirmed dog birth is twenty-three. Successive pups are usually born at irregular intervals of between half an hour and two hours, head or feet first, it doesn't matter which. Don't panic if you can't account for all the afterbirths; the bitch often eats them on the sly. Let her lick her babes and suckle them for an hour or two before you change the bedding, and don't make the new mother anxious by forcing her to go out to the toilet if she doesn't want to. Most bitches are unwilling to leave their litter at all for the first day or two, so breakfast in bed would be appreciated and toilet trips should be short and sweet. However, by about six weeks of devoted motherhood, most mongrel bitches have had enough of nursing and are feeling the pinch of needle-sharp little teeth. And most mongrel pups are fighting fit, wriggly, warm and contented. All they need is a home.

There are really very few problems to watch for, but if you notice dark green or any other brightly coloured discharge *before* the first pup is born, or if you see *no* straining, or fruitless straining for over an hour, call the vet. Similarly if a pup appears stuck halfway for more than about ten minutes, something is wrong. If you feel competent to help, grasp the puppy and pull with a smooth twist to coincide with the bitch's own movements, then clear the airways and sever the cord as already explained. Otherwise you must ask for veterinary rescue. You should also call the vet if mum fails to feed the litter or if there is continuous and pitiful crying. Otherwise leave them to get on with it. Mongrels are great survivors.

Behaviour beyond bearing

Aggression

Adopted dogs, because they come to regard their owners as saviours rather than just good friends, are prone to aggressive loyalty and jealousy. Usually this causes few problems, other than to make the owners rather conceited. However, sometimes this possessiveness causes belligerent behaviour towards other animals and other people. In this case, it always helps to lower the temperature of your relationship with the dog and share it with friends and neighbours willing to lend a hand. Very often the jealous behaviour has been secretly encouraged by the owner, who finds it rather flattering at first. Don't hug the animal to you every time someone enters the room. Encourage it to have friendly exchanges with others. Show it that the world will not actually explode if you leave it alone for half an hour. Don't let yourself become a desperate couple. If it sees another dog, don't drag it away down the road as if it were a psychopath. Let it meet its own kind. Otherwise it may form the impression, 'Four legs bad, two legs good.' Jilly Cooper's adoptive mongrel Fortnum was by inclination a great local champion who would set about neighbourhood males to show them what was what. She found that she could sometimes nip a skirmish in the bud by hiding behind a tombstone or tree so that Fortnum did not have her to defend. Fighters like this are in a small minority: most of the hundreds of mongrel owners who wrote to Jilly had peace-loving mutts; fewer than a dozen were warmongers.

If you are one of the unlucky few, examine your relationship with the dog to see if you are somehow condoning its behaviour by your devotion. Consider the advice from experts given in previous chapters for dealing with aggressive dogs. Your mongrel's status in your house should be at the bottom of the family pack, beneath your children. Most dogs accept this without much ado because, in the wild, cubs assume the rank of their parents and in wolf packs they are generally born to an august female, sired by a leading male.[4]

If your dog is unfriendly towards your children (and, as

suggested already, a bitch is much *less* likely to cause such problems), then you must get expert advice. Ask your vet to refer you to a professional like Roger Mugford, who gets 200 phone calls a month from owners, and about fifty from vets. He achieves an 83 per cent satisfaction rate – he tries to monitor it – and he specializes in behavioural problems that might, without treatment, mean a healthy dog being put down. A dog that is aggressive through jealousy and sees a member of your family as a rival for your affections may be helped by having the resented person attending to his feeding and exercise, instead of you. A treatment plan of this kind, under expert supervision, can often save the day. Status disputes between two *dogs* in the same household can generally be helped by the ruse of favouring the aggressor, rather than protecting the underdog. Try it and see. The dogs would have already worked out their mutual status to their own satisfaction by means of Chumfo between themselves, and if you try to turn this upside down, you will not prevent fights, but cause them. Greet the leading dog first, and *then* the other poor little devil to whom your heart goes out. Put the leading dog's lead on first; give him his dinner first. Don't make waves.

There are, in fact, several different types of aggression in dogs, quite apart from the possessive sort, and treatment depends upon the cause. The behaviour may have been training-induced, by someone deliberately teasing the dog. It may be pain-induced due to injury or illness, in which case you may need to apply a soft bandage muzzle while the dog is being treated. It may be fear-induced, a not uncommon cause of aggression in problem dogs. The solution is not to rain blows on the animal's head, but to calm its fears, give it a sense of security and gradually desensitize it to the source of terror.

The other common types of aggression are sexual and territorial, the same as with humans. The first may be overcome by neutering – this is *always* preferable to euthanasia or abandonment. The second, territoriality, may be evidenced by the dog causing havoc over intruders such as the gas-meter reader or Auntie May. Unfortunately this kind of aggression tends to become reinforced by the fact that many callers – the postman and the dustman, for example – go away again rather quickly and the dog thinks this is because he has seen them off. There is really no solution to this kind of 'doorbell behaviour'; indeed you may be very glad of it if you live in a neighbourhood like mine where half the passers-by are casing the joint. But dogs who are aggressive towards visitors in the house are usually those who dominate their owners anyway. The animal is simply taking responsibility as housemaster, assuming that his owner is incompetent in these matters. Territorial aggression is therefore often a matter of assuming your natural authority over the dog, as explained in a previous chapter. Otherwise you can try shutting the dog in another room at the first sign of bossy behaviour towards a visitor, until he is contrite. After a period in the cooler, he may be very glad of Auntie May's company.

Prey-chasing

Dogs will instinctively chase that which flees from them – cats, hares, stuffed hares, sheep, fowl, bicycles and even cars. The *movement away* seems to trigger the dog's predatory mechanisms, whereas a calm, seated cat will often be ignored. This is why even dogs accustomed to cats in the house will often chase spitters in the street or in the garden with unreasoning fervour. One mongrel in *Intelligent and Loyal*, attached to a table in the garden, tore it asunder in her desperation to get after her prey, and the cat was only saved by the dismembered table leg lodging in the fence as an anchor. Cats are usually quite efficient at escaping, and some will stand at bay and give the dog a taste of their claws to teach him a lesson, but livestock are often not so lucky.

I have come across all kinds of 'cures' for livestock-worrying, from shutting the dog in a ram pen, to tying a dead chicken to his tail. Obviously, fairly desperate measures are called for if your dog lives in the country and longs to kill sheep and poultry. Many lambs are mauled each year by marauding dogs, and if your mongrel is caught in the act, he may legally be shot by an irate farmer. The best insight I know into the subject comes from the German war-dog trainer, Konrad

Most, who was admittedly rather cruel in his methods. However, observe his reasoning:

> If a dog is to be prevented from killing a chicken, the correction must be given at the time when the dog has the intention of doing so. Nevertheless, the chicken he has killed can be used as a temporary expedient to stop him doing so again. While the dead bird is held close to the eyes and nose of the animal, he is given a few flicks with the switch, not by way of punishment, but in order to form the association we desire between the scent and view of the chicken and the reaction of fear in its presence provoked by the 'chicken-pain'. It would not occur to anyone whose mind works along anthropomorphic lines that such an association might be established successfully by means of a live bird *before* the dog has ever killed one. For a 'punishment prior to the crime' would, of course, be regarded by such a person as an absurdity.[5]

You may adapt this method, without using corporal punishment, for cats, sheep, or any other creature liable to be killed by your mongrel, by showing him the animal at close quarters while he is on the lead and chastising him *very* severely before he has murdered anything. If you live near a farm, there may be a sympathetic farmer only too keen to give you a hand in this worthy cause.

Destruction and digging

Digging in the garden is perfectly natural in dogs; in the wild, they are whelped underground and bitches have long racial memories of den-digging. Bone burial is another relic of the canine past. Either fence off the flowerbeds or resign yourself. It can't be 'cured'. Destruction in the house, though, is rather different, and it usually occurs for one of two reasons: boredom associated with lack of exercise, or desperation at being left alone in the house. Obviously, the first is remedied by more exercise. The best answer to the latter is 'alone' training, described in an earlier chapter. Milder forms of the disease can usually be helped by leaving the radio on when you go out, and 'barking-to-absent-friends' can sometimes be stopped by judicious use of a water pistol.

Dustbin-raking and whining

Mongrels are inveterate scavengers, and if allowed to go out unattended will go through garbage quite shamelessly – bitches as well as dogs. The answer is simple. Don't let your mongrel out without you. If he whines up a storm after reasonable exercise, get very cross indeed. Tell him that if you have any more of his nonsense you'll take him to the vet's to be *attended to*. Then ignore him altogether. When he sees he can't attract your attention by showing off, he will desist.

Muck-rolling

My mongrel Stanley is an unreclaimed ordure-roller, dropping his shoulder to many offensive substances in Epping Forest, and emerging from the brush with unspeakable stink-coats. I have no idea how to cure him and would welcome suggestions. Perhaps he should wear a plastic mac.

7

Showdown over shows

By the mid-nineteenth century in Britain, there was very high unemployment among the working breeds. Many who had toadied to man for centuries were suddenly laid off without compensation, their services rendered by new machinery. The sight of servant dogs being thrown out on their ears must have given the street mongrel pause for thought, not only about man's heartlessness but also about the already keen competition for scavengeable scraps – the mongrel's staple diet. The situation became grave indeed between 1835 and 1859 after the banning of the dog pits in which large numbers of pedigree fighters had been accustomed to earn a living tearing one another to pieces. Scarred ex-champions with cauliflower ears were thrown on to the dog dole queues. Things looked grim. Mongrels prayed, in their canine way, for deliverance from this new misery of having to share their few pathetic bits and pieces with man's working cast-offs. In 1859, their prayers were answered – or seemed to be. The first so-called Fancy Dog Show opened at Newcastle-upon-Tyne town hall, admitting pointers and setters. The mongrels thanked their lucky stars; from now on, the ex-working breeds could make their living in poofta exhibitions and freak circuses, and leave the streets to the True Dog once again. Unfortunately what the mongrels failed to realize was that with the advent of shows would come the dawn of the dog snob, and in case the mongrel had any further need to be starved, despised and denigrated, the Pure Blood brigade would now immediately attend to it.

The darker side of the show world, apart from the obvious

insolence of judging sentient creatures as though they were daubs in a gallery, was to reveal itself through a cruel hoax that rattled cashboxes all over the country. The better a dog's 'blood', and the more exclusive its ancestors, the better the price it would fetch on the open market. So myths of origin were dreamed up to account for the ancestry of particular breeds that, in truth, owed their parentage to mongrels. Historical paintings were searched for resemblances; amorphous splodges from tombstone work and ancient engravings became certain antecedents of present dogs. Incest, the only means of ensuring absolute 'purity of blood', became the rule rather than the exception, and dogs found themselves with wives who were their sisters and grandfathers who were their fathers. They became diseased and deformed.

How could such a thing be done to dogs – loving creatures after all? Well, 'breeding' is an anachronism still cherished in some joyless quarters by those who jealously guard their family trees for fear a passing mongrel may cock a leg on them. Even before the Nazis and genetic engineers threatened to make Epsilon People of humanity, the idle rich nursed their purity of blood, using coarse expressions such as 'blood will tell' in polite society. To such a mentality, fired by the advent of fancy dog competitions for the leisured classes, the mongrel was a bastard creature, whose life was nasty, brutish and short, who rummaged in refuse, did it in the streets and frightened the 'orses. The Pure Blood brigade therefore rounded on the mongrel as a beastly thing, and devised schemes for his final solution. It was they who gave the mongrel his bad name, and even today he bears its scars. Never again would True Dogs be welcomed into the company of Proper Dogs. Mongrels became – instead of the rightful summit of canine evolution – the animal anathema, the dregs of dogdom.

The first shows were farcically disorganized, like the Cremorne affair in London, involving 1200 alleged 'pedigrees' indistinguishable by the press or the judges from the mongrels in the streets, except that a lot of them had been 'faked' or tampered with, had fashionable 'dish' faces and 'strangle tongues', mutilated ears and paint-blackened noses. Many got out of their boxes and roamed the halls looking for water, losing their labels and sinking their teeth into members of the public. Early shows were often fixed. Judges were corrupt and champion dogs were poisoned by jealous exhibitors, as happened to the 'new-style' white bull terrier champion at Hull. In 1873 the Kennel Club was formed to cut down the chaos and cheating: there was a lot of money at stake. Charles Cruft, an ex-bakery boy in James Spratt's dog biscuit factory, cut his teeth as a Doggie Barnum at the Great Paris Exhibition dog show, where categories included 'Dogs Used for Human Food', 'Basset Hounds of All Kinds', 'Dogs Untamed by Man' and 'Dogs Which Become Wild'. A notable exhibit was the onomatopoeic 'Himalayan Wahh', and your mongrel would undoubtedly have won a Challenge Certificate. Exhibitors in those days were very broadminded about 'breeds' – they had to be, as there were very few off-the-peg dogs about. Champions were mostly bespoke canines, such as the enormous hippo-eared Harlequin great dane–mastiff cross who stole the 1877 Westminster Show in New York. Queen Elizabeth II's little corgi–dachshund crosses would undoubtedly have been acknowledged as a new breed, rather than debarred from Kennel Club membership as they are today, even though Her Majesty is patron of that particular outfit. Many contestants were simply freaks, with no ears, no noses, no tails. A New York exhibit had no forelimbs. The only ones apparently enjoying themselves hugely were the human exhibitors, eager to do anything to their dogs to win a prize or to own a prize freak, the canine equivalent of the fashionable Elephant Man.

Fortunately for these hapless animals, there were two guardian angels of the period in the persons of Queen Victoria and Edward VII, then Prince of Wales. Victoria deplored all cruelty to dogs and said so. She showed her own pets but stoutly refused to have anything to do with cropping or the miniaturization of poms until they could neither walk nor breed. Her Majesty's poms were big and burly. They would not be admitted to a modern pom show. The PoW, seeing the excesses of the Fancy, sucked his whiskers and entered some of his own beloved dogs in the competitions. Edward's dogs were pets and hunters, very beautiful in his estimation, and worthy to stand among champions. The great Kennel Club judge of the period, Major Harding Cox, called Edward's dogs a 'sorry lot', to which HRH responded by entering some of his more unusual ones, including two 'Indian tail-less dogs' and two 'Rampur hounds', the latter judged to be 'like small hairless deerhounds', one being 'of a mouse colour, the other spotted a sort of pink-and-blue, rather similar to young plum-pudding-coloured pigs'. They did not win prizes, but caused the judges considerable embarrassment. Things were coming to a head. Finally, losing his patience with the Fancy altogether, Edward instructed Francis Knollys to write to the Kennel Club, deploring what the Prince called 'mutilation'. 'His Royal Highness has always been opposed to this practice,' says the strongly worded letter, 'which he considers causes unnecessary suffering, and it would give him much pleasure to hear that the owners of dogs had agreed to abandon such an objectionable fashion.' Ear-cropping became a punishable offence in Britain in 1895. It continues everywhere else unabated.

The life of a modern show pedigree is not an enviable one, unless it happens to like being chalked, crimped and crated about the country, to be benched in humiliating rows, pawed and gaped at. Many show clones are sold and resold, and live out their incestuous lives in kennels, sad caricatures of working dogs now redundant. Fainting bulldogs dunked in water, boxers too nervous to eat, and terriers standing in their own filth all night, locked in boxes outside Crufts (as happened once) would no doubt give a reasonable-sized marrowbone to go with the raggle-taggle mongrels oh. All the more galling to these poor creatures is that True Dogs can enter the very *best* dog shows – the ones designed to honour dog talent and devotion, and the ones arranged purely for fun.

Decent shows

Mongrels are now definitely debarred from Crufts and all Kennel Club championship shows for fear they would eclipse the clones, but they are admitted to Exemption and Charity competitions up and down the country. Most rescue societies such as the NCDL hold their own annual dog shows. Says PR officer Clarissa Baldwin, 'We have four pedigree classes and about six or seven novelty classes that include anything from the dog with the waggiest tail to the dog with the most appealing eyes and the dog the judge would most like to take home. We get a *marvellous* response, because one of our classes is the Best Dog Rehomed from our kennels during the year, and there are generally about fifty dogs in that class.'

So if you have a particularly splendid mongrel – and who doesn't? – and you would like to show him off without showing him up, you may. Thankfully, you will not need to alter his appearance, other than to groom him respectfully as described in an earlier chapter, and the organizers of the mongrel version of Crufts, 'Scruffts', expressly request contestants to come as they are. Jilly Cooper's letters from her readers about their mongrel show-stoppers reveal that most rosettes go to rather Dougal-like 'vertical shagpiles', the wild version of Hungarian pulis with fronts similar to backs. Other bespoke champions include a Wiltshire hound, a Chiltern cheesehound, a Marsh Hatchett hound (none of these available from Harrods), and a supremely beautiful porcelain blonde with black eye-patches called Shandy Bishop. One champion whom I met, the Black Prince of Battersea, alias Blackie, is pictured in the first section of photographs wearing his rosette at an open show. Unfortunately, since those days he has let himself go slightly to seed, as ex-champs often do.

Superdogs '83

One of the most enterprising ideas for a 'new-wave' dog show was this one-off extravaganza held at Wembley Conference Centre in 1983, the brainchild of Dave and Angela Cavill of Southern Counties Dog Show, and co-organized with Vince Hogan and *Our Dogs* magazine, published since 1895 (mainly for pedigree people but embracing dogs in general). 'The show was really intended to educate people about dogs,' explains Vince Hogan, 'so whether they owned a pedigree, a show dog or a household pet, the show was aimed at them.

One of the reasons for going to Wembley, even though it cost £13,000 just to hire the shell of the building, was to upgrade the style of the dog show and enable people to watch Superdogs in relaxed circumstances. Everywhere else people are accustomed to tramping through dirty buildings or cold, wet fields to see dogs.'

What did the 4000–5000 paying customers see? Well, they saw a display team called the Pathfinders; they saw two crossbred collies belonging to Police Sergeant Gus Dermody, herding ducks; they saw a German shepherd TV star called JR; a Guide Dog called Hero; an agility display; an obedience display; Lucky, the 2.5 millionth Battersea rescue dog; 'and we also had every single breed of dog there on the day, which even Crufts or any of the Championship shows don't do because they divide them into Groups.' To educate people about frivolous pup purchase, there was a display of puppies alongside their fully grown adult versions. 'The breeders were very pleased to answer questions from pet owners. There was a great mingling of pedigree and pet people, all swopping ideas, and people with non-pedigrees at home going round the displays saying, "That looks a bit like our Spot." We didn't have any snobbery at all. We had PRO Dogs there, in the inestimable person of Lesley Scott Ordish, and we had Lucky the Battersea dog, to educate people about responsible ownership, and while the displays were going on in the main hall, we had seminars and talks in the side rooms – a vet giving information, a nutritionist, a grooming expert, and two leading show judges, Joe Braddon and Bill Siggers, explaining what they look for in a dog. It was an all-round education day.'

One of the highlights in the hall was a display by JR, coached for television by Dorothy Steves, 'to show how well-trained he was. JR can do anything – turn light switches on, operate machinery, ride a motorbike.' Then there were Floyd and Ross, the duck-herding dogs: 'That seemed to capture the imagination of the press, because Gus was outside with all these Indian runner ducks, marshalling them round the front of Wembley Conference Centre with his two crossbred collies. Very eye-catching! We wanted to broaden people's horizons about dogs; to have a show where they weren't just running around looking pretty; to show that they could work, herd sheep, guide blind people, help deaf people and actually improve human health. We generated tremendous publicity to counterbalance some of the bad press dogs have been having recently.'

What about future Superdogs? 'Superdogs '83 took three of us here four months to organize and really we're just recovering from the backlog in *Our Dogs* publishing. But the organizing company, Canine Exhibitors Ltd, is still in existence and the intention *is* to do something in the future.'

Scruffts

The Alternative Crufts – this is the Big One! It is held annually at Hewitts Farm near Orpington, Kent (*see* Appendix 6 for address and telephone number) and organized by farm-owner Geoff Rolstone and Alex Bruce, who says, 'Every dog has his day, and we feel that pedigree dogs are amply catered for up and down the British Isles, but who caters for the mongrel?' As one of the judges honoured to view the wild and woolly specimens at Scruffts each year, I can assure the Kennel Club that mongrel owners are as proud and thrilled about their dogs as any Crufts prize possessor. Marion Deeble, owner of one year's Supreme Champion, Bundle, told me, after the rigours of the ring 'He's quite posh today. He's had a bath only recently.' Bundle brought the art of scruffiness to new heights, with a striking black mop of frizzled strands surpassing any Rastafarian headpiece, the whole conveyed along by little shuffling spiders' legs that cocked deftly to flick the occasional flea into the arena. Weighed down under his enormous red, white and blue championship rosette, Bundle won his owner £500-worth of farm goodies and numerous doggie delights. 'I got him from the RSPCA South Godstone Animal Centre. All the other dogs were barking when we went in, but poor Bundle sat at the end of his cage looking mournful. He adapted to his new home straight away. Follows us everywhere. The vet says

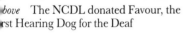

above The NCDL donated Favour, the first Hearing Dog for the Deaf

right Cross-bred Guide Dog for the Blind

Dr Roger Mugford, wearing choke chain, with his own pedigree dog wearing the Halti

Left Jilly Cooper with her beloved mongrel troop

Below Dorothy Steves with Paddy, the one-time stray who played Sandy in the West End theatre production of 'Annie'

Left Nigel Hemming's portrait of the author's pest, Stanley

Below Ex-stray Barny Grant who survived a broken leg, kennel cough and parvovirus

The Queen on beach with corgis and dorgi bringing up the rear

Right Rats on parade

Below Michael Foot with Dizzy the Tibetan Terrier, the breed often mistaken for mongrels (compare with picture of Bugsy Malone)

Ben – unwanted, like thousands more

he's about five.' What does the Supreme Champion's owner feed him on? 'Oh, Whiskas cat food. He likes Whiskas.'

Other winners parading before us were the Happiest Dog, the Dog Most Like Its Owner (two titian-haired beauties, these), the Dog with the Best Trick, the Best Obstacle Courser, the Best Tatty Pup, the Best Bone-Finder and, wait for it, the Best Lamp-post User. Alex Bruce: 'We had great difficulty borrowing the lamp-post from Bexley borough council.' Joyce Winter, proud owner of the Best Trick champion, told me that Nyde was a rescue dog, too: 'She'd been very badly beaten, with thick weals on her back, and she was petrified of the lead.' Now Nyde does tricks for chocolate drops, counting to three and shaking hands, and her girth is anything but sylph-like, quite unlike her former self. 'She was like something out of Belsen when I got her. Skin and bone,' says Joyce Winter.

Alex Bruce reflected on how Scruffts got off the ground in 1983: 'Regardless of how po-faced we were about the thing, it soon degenerated into what it was meant to be – a shambles. I'd run a similar show in Devon previously, and that was frightening because at 2.30 when it was scheduled to start we had four dogs. But as soon as I announced to the village "Apple Pie Fair" that the dog show was about to commence, car doors burst open everywhere and people began dragging out all different shapes and sizes. A shambles inevitably occurs in the collection ring – they're not exactly well-behaved.' Whatever gave them the idea? Has Alex got a mongrel? 'I've got a rough collie, and people ask me why I don't show him. Well, (a) he fancies his chances enough as it is, and (b) his ears have collapsed. I wouldn't want to show him anyway. If he's happy with his lugs, so am I.' Hewitts Farm, the largest fruit-and-veg-picking farm in Europe, has mounted publicity stunts for charity in the past, with the world's biggest apple pie, weighing 13.66 tonnes, and 'Strawberries for the Falklands' during the war. But Scruffts took even Geoff Rolstone by surprise. 'We never expected it to, but it got publicity all over the country.' Hewitts Farm did, in fact, have a dog, a lazy, egg-sucking mongrel called Rasters. Says Alex, 'We wanted him on the lead in the ring to set a good example, but he objected. Ignored the obstacle course altogether, apart from getting lost in the sausage tunnel. We thought perhaps he'd lain down and fallen asleep, so I did a rough imitation of a Southern drawl and shouted out, "Rasters! Come on out of there!" as part of my commentary. He went on to win Best Lamp-post User, as though he'd been trained.'

The first Supreme Champion was Bugsy Malone. Scruffts Judge Jenny Kearney, owner of East Lodge Grooming: 'We spotted that dog before he even got to that part of the competition. It was without doubt the scruffiest dog we'd seen. You see, although Scruffts is principally for mongrels, it isn't exclusively, and you can get some jolly scruffy pedigrees. Bugsy was one.' The first champion was therefore not a mongrel, but a Tibetan terrier. Said Alex Bruce, 'Look at the state of him. The fellow from the *Daily Express* honestly didn't know which end was which till the dog started panting and you could just make out this small pink arc.' Oddly enough, Michael Foot's dog Dizzy, much-publicized nibbler of discarded Romany chicken bones on Hampstead Heath, is of the same ilk. Mr Foot wrote to me, 'I have to tell you that he is not a mongrel. Not that I have anything against mongrels. But he is in fact a Tibetan terrier and we did get him because he reminded us of another dog we used to have.' Betty Fincham and young Lindsay Roebotham, jointly the proud exhibitors of Bugsy Malone, have the same problem. Mrs Fincham: 'They're ugly little pups, Tibetan terriers, and my husband said, "You must be mad paying all that money. It's an old mongrel!" But then there must be hundreds of old mongrels as lovely as he is – they're all lovable. Anyway, we only popped into Hewitts Farm to get some strawberries and we saw the show was for "non-pedigrees", so I told Lindsay that Bugs wouldn't qualify. But the fellow on the door said, "Well, I've seen Heinz 57 varieties, and that's the worst." So he let us in. I was bloody annoyed actually because I thought, "I've paid a lot of money for him"! He's very comical. He can't lie down in the garden – he has to have his bum in a deckchair. He meets a hedgehog at night on the lawn, and he kisses the horses at the bottom of the garden.' Lindsay: 'He's a bit of a nuisance though when you're trying to groom him because he jumps up and down a lot. Betty has a selection of brushes for different bits of him, but he doesn't look any different. He actually won a prize to be cut for the summer, but it didn't work out quite as expected.' Alex Bruce: 'Yes, he got doggie chops, Bonios and a free grooming at East Lodge Grooming, but Thames TV got in touch with them saying they wanted him, *scruffy*, on this show. Where was he? He was at the grooming parlour! Lindsay rang the police. "My mother's taken this dog to be groomed, and he's on the telly tomorrow. Could you stop them grooming him?" ' So the police went screaming round Biggin Hill looking for this parlour and got there literally as the girl was about to put the comb into the back of his head. "'Allo, 'allo, 'allo – this is the place. Don't groom that dog!" shouted the police, and Jenny thought "Hell's teeth. A bent dog at Scruffts. Somebody's running a hot-dog racket!"

8

Limelight and mongrels

Mongrels are not new to show business. Along with poodles and terriers, they have been hopping and jigging to music in streets and circuses since time immemorial, turning somersaults and pirouettes in soiled finery, plumed hats and ruffs. The art is as old as begging itself, and the choreographer often as harsh. Nobel Prize-winning ethologist Konrad Lorenz, who disapproves of dog-degeneration by breeders and crosses chows with German shepherds to produce wolfy types, has observed that circus dogs around the world that perform complex tricks are rarely pedigrees. He says this is because mongrels are more intelligent and less nervous.[1] Sir Walter Scott commented, 'The *garçon perruquier* and his bare-bottomed, red-eyed poodle. . . are both amusing animals and play 10,000 tricks that are diverting enough; yet there is more of human and dog-like sympathy in the wag of old Trusty's tail than if his rival Toutou had stood on his head for a twelvemonth.'

These days, mongrel performers are very much in demand for theatre, television and film work. A most unusual recent audition was undoubtedly the one to replace stage-frightened actor Bertie, the vicar's dog in the farce *See How They Run* at the Shaftesbury Theatre. Thirty-eight hopefuls were auditioned, including a setter, some German shepherds, a couple of pekes and Fred Basset, the real-life dog of the cartoon strip's creator Alex Graham. But the part starring opposite John Alderton went to Boot, a mongrel of enormous personal charm, stage presence and curly whiskers, who belongs to thirteen-year-old Saskia Porter. Another mongrel thespian is Dougal (the real dog, not the animated floormop in *Magic Roundabout*), like Boot a shaggy brunette Heinz belonging to actor David King. Dougal has done Shakespeare, Chekhov, *Toad of Toad Hall* and suitable television work. He gets a very fine write-up in Jilly Cooper's book, *Intelligent and Loyal*, where we discover that, as a youngster, he had a tendency to rip people's homes up. David King was, in fact, his fifth owner in as many months; they met at the Haymarket Theatre, and it was here that Dougal eventually had a change of heart about delinquency and pledged his life to an acting career. His Moonshine in *Midsummer Night's Dream* received rave notices, three Shin Bone Nominations and a Chocolate Bar Award. Usually he sits in the green room while his master is on stage, but he once wandered out in the middle of a performance of *Henry IV*, hearing Glendower's boast about calling forth spirits from the vasty deep.

Speaking of vasty deeps, the big screen has seen many a mongrel bit part, especially in films set in an historical context before clones were considered the thing, and a plump brown ship's mongrel in *The Bounty* captures everyone's eye in the storm scenes, playing a frightened old sea dog. She loyally lets out a squeal to warn Bligh of the midnight skulduggery below decks, and leaps from her hammock to tell Anthony Hopkins all, despite one of the mutineers trying to hold her jaws shut. Doleful Dolores, an ex-Battersea girl with a smattering of spaniel, actually received quite serious critical acclaim for her part in Graham Greene's 1957 film, *Across the Bridge*, starring opposite Rod Steiger. One of her press cuttings is from the *News Chronicle*:

> The latest portrait in Rod Steiger's small but unforgettable rogues' gallery is the fugitive crook-financier of *Across the Bridge*. You may gauge the portrait's brilliance by the fact that its perpetrator just succeeds in stealing the picture from one of the most endearing bitches in screen-history – a mournfully unthoroughbred spaniel called Dolores, who was discovered in Battersea Dogs' Home and groomed specifically for co-stardom with Mr Steiger. St Sebastian never gazed skyward with so monumental a look of martyrdom as Dolores in her final anguish. Landseer never found a sitter whose nose was more moist with devotion. Had the film been a silent one, she might have queened it over all comers; but though she

can snarl and yelp and whimper as evocatively as any exponent of
The Method, she cannot speak – and here Mr Steiger has the
measure of her.[2]

Walt Disney, who knew a thing or two about cinema
audiences, crafted the character of his brave scavenging mutt
in *Lady and the Tramp* to make a point about pedigree snobbery.
This cartoon is as near to social satire as Disney ever chose to
go. The story ends with the mongrel vindicated, having suc-
cessfully wooed both his purebred spaniel girlfriend and her
snotty family, who buy him a licence. The crossbred pups
comprise three spaniel types and one unreclaimed grey scruffbag that is the spitting image of his embourgeoised father.

Disney could convey any emotion through the medium of
his humanized animals, but how do you actually get a real dog
to act? As Barbara Woodhouse told me, without difficulty.
Overseas, 99 per cent of the dogs she trains are mongrels from
the shelters, hoping to get them homes through their TV work,
and even as a lass she used to go out with mutts on leads and
RSPCA collecting tins. 'It entirely depends on the training of a
dog as to whether it reacts with pleasure when acting. The
praise it gets when it does right matters so much. Dogs very
much sense an important occasion which, of course, acting is.
If kindly trained, I believe dogs look forward to this type of
work,' says Mrs Woodhouse. Indeed, American mongrel film
star Benji had a whole TV documentary devoted to his
skills, and his descendant, Pippin, is famous in her own right
in the UK.

Dorothy Steves has been training animal television stars for
many years, has 120 dogs on her books, coached Radar in
Softly, Softly and JR, her current German shepherd prodigy, can
operate a computer with his paws. In fact, most of the dog
television actors these days seem to have been trained by
Dorothy Steves, including the cast of *Wuffer*. She believes there
is now a trend away from pedigrees towards mongrels in
cinema and television: 'It isn't just a question of temperament;
physically in many ways, pedigree dogs have been changed by
judges who seem determined to destroy what is natural and
good for the sake of a temporary fad. Many people believe

there will be a new set of "breeds" before too long. Mongrels are a great race of beings, and as you know, I've rescued several motley mixes and they've all come through 1000 per cent. One has to be prepared to cope with whatever bad habits they have acquired, or the results of bad treatment they have been subjected to, but after that they seem to remember for life that it was *you* who rescued them. My newest "Mickey", who was in the musical *Peg*, is as great an example as "Sandy" from *Annie*. The TV series I'm now making for children has two of its six episodes devoted to mongrels and ex-inmates of dog pounds.' Dorothy trains her dog stars by telepathy, kindness and hand-signals and treats. 'I sometimes have literally ten minutes to prepare a dog for some fantastic stunt, but I refuse to do anything that has to be faked with tranquillizers. A dog can so easily be taught to act these things; they have a very great sense of occasion, and when a trainer has a direct line to their minds and feelings, there's nothing they can't do.' She feels very strongly that animal actors in TV studios should be protected from the whims of heartless directors, which at the moment they are not, and she doesn't train dogs for advertising – 'that is boring and sometimes cruel – all day long repeating stupid tiny little shots. What I do has to involve a dog's intelligence.' Fortunately, since products are generally pushed by up-market pedigrees with snob value, mongrels until recently haven't been in demand in the advertising world anyway.

The roguery and individuality of mongrels seems to endear them particularly to people in show business, perhaps because inside every great star there's a mongrel trying to get out. Edmund Kean, the hell-raising nineteenth-century tragedian thought to be the greatest of them all, used to raise Cain backstage even as a youngster. His guardian put a dog collar round his neck inscribed, 'BRING THIS BODY TO MISS TIDSWELL.' We don't know whether he had a licence or not. Jeremy Irons, filming *Brideshead Revisited* at Castle Howard in Yorkshire, used to look across the landscape and see his adopted Battersea mongrel Speed racing about in all his glory. Speed has died now but Jeremy once told me, 'Speed is now ten and I have had him for nine years. Being a mongrel, he has of course a great deal more intelligence than any pedigree dog, which makes it easier for him since his life is very changeable due to my career, and he must be very adaptable. He has spent many hours with me in rehearsal rooms and on film sets and in dressing rooms. He used to ride on the back of my motorcycle with me and is trained so that he never needs to be on a lead. He is a cross between, as far as one can tell, a Staffordshire bull terrier and a pointer and there must be some collie somewhere since he handles sheep with great professionalism. He has flown many times with me to Ireland and he is a wonderful guard dog.'

The late Pat Phoenix, immortalized as Elsie Tanner in *Coronation Street*, once owned a timber wolf called Blackie who opened doors by knocking them down. Her home outside Manchester, Sunny Place Cottage, was totally given over to a menagerie of four pekes and a mongrel called Sally. Pat had a tiled floor and thought twice before she bought any posh furniture. As she once said, 'I saw a lovely Georgian sort of suite the other week, a lovely Chinese blue, in velvet it was, and I was just about to buy it and I thought what's the point? The dogs would ruin it. It's like having kids that never get past three years of age.'[3] They all slept in Pat's bedroom on their own cushions, 'which could be a hazard to your relationships at times, but they're family!' The family consisted of Sam, Scottie, Sophie and Chips, all pekes, and Sally. 'She's a mongrel. Some kids came to the front door one day with this disgusting little object in their arms with bald eyes, stinking of diesel oil, rickets and God knows what else. These puppies had been born under a farm tractor. The farmer was shooting them, as they do, you see. They'd got black labradors and scotties in the litter, they said, and this was the last of the scotties!' Pat's cousin Kitty, the housekeeper, was anguished and told her in floods of tears that these pups were going to be shot. 'So I said to her, oh for God's sake take it in! That's Sally. She's a professional coward, but she had a bad start. No one ever raises their voice when Sally's around.'

There are mongrels in many another well-known homestead. Actor Peter Bowles has an ex-Battersea cross collie/Old English sheepdog. Bernie Winters' enormous spayed St Bernard, Snorbitz, who lumbered up to me recently at a veterinary congress, has an impeccable pedigree and has, Bernie whispers tactfully, 'never been touched', but she was not Bernie's first pet: he had a mongrel called Lou for sixteen years who was a great personal friend. Pop star and author Alvin Stardust has a mongrel called Gracie, adopted by his ex-wife, actress Liza Goddard and son Thomas from Battersea. Newscaster Richard Whitmore adopted his mongrel from the Blue Cross kennels at Kimpton Bottom in Hertfordshire, and Janet Ledger the painter has a glossy black shadow called Simon, featured in many of her paintings and in two of her lithographs at the Tate. The best buddy cartoonist Jack Fish ever had was a white scruffbag called Bill, to whom he was so devoted as a boy that he made up his mind to commemorate the dog in his cartoons. Bill has now appeared in at least 1700 of them. Author and journalist Jilly Cooper, mongrel standard-bearer, became hooked on Heinzes after acquiring her first rescued one, Fortnum the feisty, and taking in Mable and Barbara soon afterwards to give him a sense of harem majesty. Jilly wrote to me, 'I'm absolutely enchanted to hear you are doing a book on mongrels. I'm a huge fan as you know, and, as you also say, we are competing against frightening ignorance and bigotry.' Jilly's *Intelligent and Loyal: A Celebration of the Mongrel* contains news of hundreds of mongrels whose owners wrote in proudly to tell Jilly about their dogs raising two claws to the Kennel Club and cocking a leg at pedigree prejudice. The stories, sad and funny, are required reading for all mongrel-lovers, and the one that adheres most particularly to the memory concerns Evans, who belonged to Jilly's own paternal grandfather and who was apparently so ugly that the gardener thought he should have been named after the other place. 'Despite his hellish aspect, however,' writes Ms Cooper, 'Evans had a lovely nature, and was so intelligent that he managed simultaneously to drink out of the lavatory and hold the door open with his tail so it wouldn't shut him in.'[4]

Politicians are not renowned for their devotion to mongrels but then perhaps politicians instinctively prefer the sort of pedigree dogs associated with the farmyard. However, Jeremy Corbyn, MP for Islington North, is very proud of his bitzer, and so is Icelandic Finance Minister Albert Gudmundsson, owner of a mongrel bitch called Lucy, aged thirteen. Iceland has in operation a currish law banning dogs from its cities and Mr Gudmundsson was reported to Reykjavik police for keeping Lucy in defiance. He replied angrily, 'Lucy is a dear member of our family, as dear to us as a child. We will never agree to part with her. Rather we will emigrate from Iceland and I will quit politics.' Ironically, the year after the Icelandic dog ban, in 1925, the inhabitants of Nome, Alaska were saved from being wiped out by diphtheria by dog teams running serum through the blizzards: such is the gratitude for canine service to Arctic humanity. The most eminent political dog in the United Kingdom, of course, was Lord Hailsham's own Spotty Dog, who used to accompany Lord Hailsham, when he was Lord Chancellor on his visits to the House of Lords. Spotty Dog, a Jack Russell-ish little character with needle-sharp teeth, had been known to nibble a few noble ankles but left the Lord Chancellor's wig alone, as well as his woolsack.

One mongrel who has seen it all is the unspeakably gorgeous Bothie, the small fiery scruffbag who accompanied Sir Ranulph Fiennes and his wife on their Polar 'Transglobe Expeditions'. Bothie has wetted on both Poles without altering the earth's magnetic balance, wears woollies and balaclavas that would not disgrace Captain Scott and is estimated to have travelled about 52,000 miles (83,200 km) circumnavigating the globe. He has fought with moose in the Yukon, seen off wolves in white wastelands and told penguins what he thought of them in the Antarctic. 'A mongrel he undoubtedly is,' says Ranulph Fiennes, 'and a stubborn-minded, non-housetrained, contrary-souled, yappy-voiced one at that. But he is also Bothie who made us laugh and gave us something to love and talk to during those long, difficult months.'[5] Bothie marks his territory indoors and out and bathes in the Thames all year round.

Despite the boorish snobbery that mongrels have endured from some ill-inbred sections of society, they have indeed lain at the hearths of stately homes around the world. Society columnist Nigel Dempster summed it up in an article 'In and Out' in the *Sunday Telegraph Magazine*, in which he noted that certain popular fashions breeds were now 'out' and

Battersea mongrels now 'in'. Margaret, a tender white Battersea stray with black eye-rims, travelled out to Abu Dhabi by private jet to become the darling of an oil sheikh, and two others were flown to Geneva to join the household of a Sudanese ruler with territories larger than the British Isles. The Duke of Beaufort, Battersea's late President, paid regular visits to the home with the Duchess, and several strays went off with them to live in splendour, as Baroness Gloria Cottesloe puts it, 'to grace – and, to a large degree, to rule – the ducal home at Badminton.'[6] A mongrel appears in the coat of arms of the Phillips family of Stoke d'Abernon Manor in Surrey to honour the dog who saved ancestor William Phillips in 1789 from drowning in Portsmouth harbour. But the crowning glory, so far as posh homes go, must be moving in with royalty.

A mongrel acquaintance of Henry VIII, for example, merely altered the course of history. Of unknown parentage and non-spaniel aspect, she belonged to Henry's emissary to the Vatican to procure an annulment of his marriage with Catherine of Aragon. As the emissary (the Earl of Wiltshire according to some accounts) observed protocol by bending to kiss the Pope's toe, his Holiness made the mistake of moving his foot forward. The bitch, seeing this gesture, seized the papal foot, and a 'riotous' scene ensued. Henry VIII, unable to secure his divorce, founded the Church of England, and the little mongrel was presumably declared 'excommunicate and anathema'. King Charles II, spaniels notwithstanding, loved his own mongrel, a black dog 'between a greyhound and a spaniel' (which could mean just about anything). One day it went missing and the King offered a sizeable reward to anyone fetching it back, as he was very upset and believed it had been stolen. The dog wouldn't have wandered off, the King reasoned, as it loved him dearly and, in any case, it wasn't English.

So-called 'pedigrees' belonging to members of the Royal Family have often been of the inadmissible-to-the-Kennel-Club sort. King Charles' own spaniels looked quite different from the strange little squash-faced fellows now masquerading under the title, as you may see from paintings and the display of early specimens in Tring Zoological Museum. Indeed, few royal portraits contain anything Crufty at all. Edward VII's 'French bulldog' Peter and 'fox terrier' Caesar were of the type to catch the judge's boot rather than his eye, and Marco, the so-called 'golden pom' belonging to Queen Victoria, weighed 30 lb (13.6 kg), looked more like a keeshond, and was called by Her Majesty a 'spitz' rather than a tiddly pom. Her childhood pet 'Dash', with whom she appears as a girl in R. Westall's portrait, has been claimed as either a dachshund or a Manchester terrier, and even Mary Queen of Scots' little black-and-white pet, found hidden in her skirts after her execution, has been variously described as a 'spaniel' and a 'Skye terrier' – such is the confusion of claims over early 'breeds'. At least in the US White House, things are more straightforward. No bones were made about Amy Carter's merry mongrel, named by the peanut family with surprising imagination after a cereal – 'Grits'.

However, the highest accolade for non-pedigree chums 'by appointment' must go to Piper and Chipper, crossbreds to Her Majesty Queen Elizabeth II. Piper is a dorgi bitch and Chipper a dorgi dog, the only male member of the heel-nipping entourage. These little creatures are the fruit of a liaison between Princess Margaret's miniature long-haired dachshund dog Pipkin and female members of the Queen's Pembroke corgi dynasty, all descended from her eighteenth birthday present, Susan. They are very nice little dogs, and the first pups so captivated the Royal Family that Pipkin was forgiven and allowed to father some more. His characteristics feature very strongly in his offspring, his long hair inherited by his daughter Piper. Chipper is smooth-haired, like a corgi. The troupe live handsomely as you might expect, feeding on rabbit from the royal parks – Piper and Chipper excel at locating game – and travelling by car, train and plane between the Queen's residences at Buckingham Palace, Windsor Castle, Balmoral and Sandringham. Eat your heart out, Crufts' champions.

Some mongrels on whom the limelight has fallen have not

been show business personalities, royal pets or dogs-about-town, but the sad victims of unwanted publicity. Such a one was Trixie, a chocolate-coloured, watery-eyed little rough-coat currently staying at the NCDL kennels at Wichenford, Hereford & Worcester, with all the other strays. When her mistress Hilda Harris died, Trixie became the main beneficiary of her will, inheriting £27,000 in memory of a great friendship. Mrs Harris's brother, an ex-bus-driver, commented, 'It's an insult. If the money had gone to a medical charity, I would say good luck, but this bequest for a dog is ridiculous.'[7] While the legal wrangles continue, Trixie lives out her days like the stray she was when Mrs Harris adopted her. All *she* wants is a home.

9
Mongrel service

Although mongrels originally declared themselves independent over the issue of dog labour, and although they declined to have their genes reorganized for work like the pedigree drudges, they are perfectly capable of lending a paw in a crisis. Eccentric and unbowed they may be, and too intelligent to be bothered with silly routine jobs, but in times of genuine distress and trouble, when war, or old age, disability or despair have laid somebody low, mongrels have been prompt enough to offer their quick-witted affection, to labour and not to ask for any reward, save that of knowing they did man's will. At the heart of Edinburgh Castle, among tributes to the glorious dead in the Scottish National War Memorial, are the records of animals who gave their lives in two world wars, bearing the inscription, 'Remember also the humble beasts that served and died.' Canine combatants in the First World War alone, by one estimate, totalled over 75,000 – sentries, wire-layers, mine-detectors, guards, haulage dogs and messengers – brave mongrels serving alongside brave pedigrees. A *Times* report of September 1917 refers to the untrained dogs of northern France and Flanders, sent like lambs to the slaughter: 'It is the dogs who enlist men's sympathy more than anything else. Like frightened children they joined the ranks, nestling down by the side of the men for warmth and protection. Their piteous eyes seem to ask, What does it all mean? What has happened to the world?'

The British were among the last Europeans to enlist dogs during the world wars, setting up a school at Shoeburyness in 1916 under Colonel Edward Richardson. The dogs' homes were combed for 'volunteers' and conscientious objectors sent to the lethal chamber at Battersea. Colonel Richardson, himself an Airedale breeder, protests in his book *British War Dogs*, 'A very general idea prevails, that only mongrels have any real sense of cleverness,' but of course there were clever purebred dogs, too (he mentions a collie, Nell, as an example). To begin with, Colonel Richardson had posted a couple of Airedales, and also a crossbred sheepdog that went to the Eighth Gurkha Regiment for the Abor campaign in India, and these being successful, the training programme now got underway for the trenches. The War Office appealed to the public to donate a dog for Britain, and the response was 'exceedingly generous'. Dogs of all breeds came flooding in, and many mongrels 'of humble ancestry nevertheless came with wise faces and willing hearts'. Once they got over their homesickness and bewilderment at their owners' 'exceeding generosity', they went into testing and training as 'messengers', 'sentries' or 'guards'.

The messengers with their canister collars saved many lives, not only of human runners, but of whole units whose fate hung in the messages round the dogs' necks. They were unswerving when lines were down, capable of great speed over unfamiliar terrain even at night, and presented only a small target under heavy bombardment. Keeper Osbourne reported the invaluable work of a little crossbred spaniel-retriever type called Jim, giving early warning of mustard gas by his behaviour, and then running with a warning message to HQ, arriving three-quarters of an hour before the alert sent by wire. 'When gas is about,' wrote Osbourne, 'I have to see to the putting of Jimmy's head in a man's PH smoke helmet, and I should be greatly pleased if you could inform me where to secure a mask for his proper protection.' Many sheepdogs, collies, drovers' dogs and lurchers were used for this dangerous job, 'as well as all crosses of the above'. Poodles messed about; greyhounds proved useless and hounds were not interested in the work at all. Neither were dogs with curly tails. 'This method of carrying the tail,' says Richardson, 'seems to indicate a certain levity of character.' Messengers were trained to return to a handler three or four miles away, through shell-holes, mud, smoke, barbed wire, gas, gunfire, thunderflash bombs, eighteen-pounder artillery guns and twelve-inch 'heavies'. There were also 'liaison dogs' trained to make the hazardous double journey to the Front and back between two handlers, involving heavier canine casualties.

Seven thousand war dogs *officially* lost their lives, but many more were gassed, burned and blown away. Their rations were three-quarters of a pound of bread or broken biscuit with half a pound of horseflesh per dog per day. When they perished they were unmourned by any but their handlers, and the job of bringing back survivors after the war had to be undertaken by the RSPCA. This was all the thanks Britain's dog soldiers received – first-rate recruits, not only as messengers, but guards, sentries, draught-dogs, search dogs, scouts, reconnaissance dogs, wire-layers, ambulance and rescue dogs, mine-detectors, parachutists and, in World War II, ARP (Air-Raid Precautions) dogs, finding casualties who would otherwise have remained buried under air-raid rubble. Many who gave their lives would not have been admitted to the Kennel Club, supposing they had wished to so demean themselves.

Holders of the dog VC during World War II – the Dickin Medal awarded by the PDSA 'For gallantry – we also serve' – were commemorated in a recent exhibition at the Imperial War Museum in London, along with other animal war recruits. A large proportion of medallists seem to be mongrels and crossbreeds, such as Rickie, the mine-detector who served in Holland, France and Belgium; Brian, the German shepherd cross parachute dog with the 13th Battalion Airborne Division; Rob, the patrol mongrel with the SAS in North Africa and Italy who parachuted behind enemy lines with recce parties; and Gypsy, the first serving English dog to cross the Rhine and the Elbe, decorated by the Dutch government and eventually lamed in an air-raid. Another mongrel medallist, Bob, served in North Africa, Sicily and Italy, and saved his patrol from a night ambush.

Then there were the ARP dogs – such as scruffy little Rip, who became the mascot of the ARP at Poplar, hunting for signs of life undetectable to the human ear or eye – and the mascots at home and abroad, who raised morale by seeming unaffected in a crisis: mongrels such as Benghazi Ben of the Royal Army Service Corps, Tich of the First Battalion, King's Royal Rifle Corps, Sandy, ship's mongrel to the *Ark Royal*, and Peggy, the knee-throb of HMS *Amethyst*: official reports acknowledge what a difference they made in keeping men's peckers up. Even the National Fire Brigade had a mongrel mascot, called Ben – 'a regular little cockney', according to his superiors, and 'sharp as a needle'. Dog mascots are as old as war. Queen Victoria is said to have wept over one called Bobby who, after surviving the Battle of Maiwand in Afghanistan in 1880, met his death under a carriage. And many have shed a tear for the most famous of them all, little Moustache, born in Calais in 1799 to march to the sound of the drum. Moustache joined up of his own accord with a parade of Grenadiers, deserting his grocer owner. An ugly, dirty little tyke, he weaseled his way into favour by marking time with his dishevelled feet. It took him three weeks to learn proper marching, and after that there was no stopping him. One day, however, a chasseur, mistaking him for some local scrounger, hit Moustache a glancing blow with the flat of his sabre, which caused the dog to dissociate himself from the regiment and join up with some dragoons, whom he followed into Spain. He was eventually killed by a cannonball at the battle of Badajos, and buried with full military honours, collar, medal and all. A small monument was placed over his grave, but the Spaniards dug it up and burned his bones.

A latter-day mongrel mascot, Rats, is still alive and kicking after serving five years in Crossmaglen on the Northern Ireland/Eire border with the British Army, longer than any other soldier. D777 Rats is a short, stocky, prick-eared little perpetrator with a stump of a tail, not from docking, but from a fire bomb. A fellow-soldier says of him, 'He was an oasis of friendship in a desert of sadness.'[1] Rats has now retired from active service on veterinary advice, to concentrate his mind on fatherhood. In fact, he has already sired four daughters and two sons by a couple of local girls, Badger and Boodle, a change from getting in and out of Saracen trucks. Not that a mongrel can ever forget the excitement of Ulster, or the full dress parade of the First Battalion the Welsh Guards, or his war-wounds, or the bomb splinters buried in his tough little frame. He has put it all in his memoirs, dictated to Max Halstock and called *Rats: the story of a dog soldier*.[2]

Anyone who thinks crossbreeds cannot be trained to the highest degree is mistaken. Take Guide Dogs, for example. Now, the Guide Dogs for the Blind Association (GDBA) have a famously successful breeding programme, based at Tollgate House near Warwick. Some 165 brood bitches are looked after by volunteers in their own homes and then at six weeks old the puppies are placed with puppy-walking families, who provide basic training for the first year of their lives. After this the young dogs go to one of the seven GDBA training centres for a futher seven to nine months' work.

In the 1930s in Britain, the original Guide Dogs were GSDs, but as these were needed for military duties during the war, collies, sheepdogs, keeshonds, retrievers, boxers *and* cross-breeds were used. The breeding programme began in the 1950s to make selection less random. About half of modern British Guide Dogs are labradors, though in Germany where the scheme's organization began, and in the United States where the demand for 'seeing eye' dogs is great, German shepherds are preferred, along with dobermanns. Says the PR manager of Britain's GDBA, 'Now, as regards whether or not we use cross-breeds, the answer is yes. A good number of Guide Dogs are labradors crossed with golden retrievers; this has proved a very successful cross. We also try out new crosses from time to time, such as the border collie crossed with a golden retriever, with which we are having some good results. Also, a small number of Guide Dogs come from outside sources as opposed to our own breeding scheme, and a few of these will be cross-breeds.' It is very expensive to train each animal, and the GDBA rely entirely on public donations. Guide Dogs have been in existence since blind people, and a wall painting from Herculaneum (on the site of modern Resina in Italy) dated to the time of Christ shows a blind beggar with an old mutt on a lead, as do a number of medieval woodcuts. The Viennese Joseph Reisinger, who had a Guide Dog coached for him in the 1780s by the Quinze-Vingts hospital in Paris and who trained his replacements himself, wasn't particular about what the dog looked like, so long as it would learn. His first 'eyes' belonged to a spitz. The NCDL have provided several excellent modern non-pedigrees for GDBA training, among them a beautiful cross samoyed called Scouse from their Kenilworth centre. The NCDL offer these dogs as a fitting rejoinder to 'those sceptics who say that all abandoned dogs should be destroyed'.[3]

Around the world, scientists are waking up to the importance of companion animals to human health. A recent international symposium on the subject in Vienna had speakers from both sides of the Iron Curtain. Dr Aaron Katcher of the University of Pennsylvania summed up current research by saying, 'Companion animals have the capacity to calm their owner into a kind of reverie.' This 'reverie' has a beneficial effect on blood pressure, on recovery from heart attack, and on the ability to withstand stress. Dogs have been introduced into homes and hospitals to help the criminally insane, alcoholics, agoraphobics, the retired, the elderly, the lonely and the depressed, and to draw withdrawn children into contact with the outside world. Researchers are becoming very excited about the possibilities, and one leading authority predicts that doctors will soon routinely prescribe a dog rather than a drug.[4]

Losing a companion animal is hurtful and may occasionally lead to pathological depression. Being deliberately deprived of one by being placed in an institution is a fate worse than death to many of the elderly people languishing in homes, who regarded their animals as their close friends. Schemes to combat this cruel and unnatural state of affairs are underway in the United States, Britain, Australia and Canada, where animals are being introduced into wards to make them more like home. (You might mention this next time somebody complains about *toxocara canis*!) Recently a man in Southampton General Hospital came out of a coma because he heard the bark of his dog Tipper tethered outside his hospital window. Another patient, at Shelton psychiatric hospital in Shropshire, was saved from pining away by being allowed to have his dog Nell in residence. PRO Dogs National Charity have launched a scheme in the UK called PAT Dogs – 'PRO Dogs Active Therapy Dogs' – offering volunteer members covered by their insurance scheme the chance to share their dogs once a week or once a fortnight with people in institutions. Old folk close their eyes and weep for joy to hold a dog in their arms again. If your mongrel is reasonably well-behaved and friendly and would like to be made a fuss of, find out more by writing to Lesley Scott Ordish, Founder, PRO Dogs (*see* Appendix 6 for address). PAT Dogs are already visiting in Oxford, Essex, Hereford, London, Kent and Derbyshire, cheering up children, disabled people and old folk who couldn't be bothered to speak before they came.

My book on canine services to humanity, *Your Obedient Servant* (Century Hutchinson), celebrated many a mongrel worker among the spitwheel-turners, truffle-hunters, space-travellers, rat-catchers, witch-finders, lace-smugglers and hunting, hauling and rescue dogs. Did you know, for example, that the Zorastrians of ancient Persia revered stray mutts as local cleansing officers and protected them by religious ordinances in the *Zend-Avesta*? But pride of place among mongrel service dogs, I think, must go to a new branch of workers, the Hearing Dogs for the Deaf, the British and American ex-strays from the shelters who have, without benefit of pedigree, rescued people from a silent prison.

There are 14 million people in the United States who are hard of hearing, and deafness strikes one in five people in Britain. For the rest of their lives, sufferers are walled into a strange and soundless world where they can become suspicious, dependent and lonely – visitors ring the doorbell and go away, and very often they don't come back. Since 1976 in the USA, over 200 mutts, most of them from the dogs' homes, have been trained as 'hearing aids' for the deaf, living in their houses and flats and rushing to fetch them to the source of a sound, such as the kettle whistling, the doorbell, the baby crying or the ring of the amplified telephone. In 1982, the Royal National Institute for the Deaf employed ex-police dog trainer Tony Blunt, who went to America to study the techniques and adapted them here.

The prototype British Hearing Dog was Favour, a mongrel provided, like many more, by the NCDL. PR Officer Clarissa Baldwin: 'They're all mongrels, and we're delighted because it does mean that the dogs go to jolly good homes where people are really going to appreciate them.' I was privileged to meet Favour, a magnolia-coloured, gentle creature with freckled legs, now used for demonstration purposes, and some of the other pioneer dogs such as Chum, a shiny black cross labrador who has altered the lives of James and Isabella Chapman, both profoundly deaf. Said Isabella, 'Chum will give us that bit more confidence to cope.'

With the advent of welcome sponsors such as Pedigree Petfoods, a couple of pedigree labradors and a chihuahua have got in on the act, but the original Hearing Dogs and the mainstay of the scheme have been mongrels. Co-founder Bruce Fogle told me, 'All the dogs in training right now or that have been trained are mongrels. Chum happens to be a cross labrador, but the first Dog, Favour – there's no conceivable way you could figure out what he is!' How are they trained? Programme controller Tony Blunt: 'It costs about £2500 to train each dog and it takes four months. What I do first of all is to go to the deaf person's home and make recordings of particular sounds they'd like to be alerted to – I think a dog can learn five or six before getting into problems – then I put myself in all the situations that I think the deaf person might be in, like washing up at the kitchen sink, and when the dog hears the recording, he must come and touch me on the leg and take me to the source of the sound. He must make contact – you ignore him till he does.'

The new Hearing Dogs for the Deaf Centre at Chinnor, Oxfordshire (*see* Appendix 6 for address and telephone number), is funded entirely on donations. The dogs give deaf people a new 'lease on life', a companion, a clue to what's going on in the world, and a friend to nudge them or lick their arms in the mornings when the alarm goes off. Does Mr Blunt plan to breed Hearing Dogs, like Guide Dogs for the blind? 'No. We tried that when I was in the police service and look at the cost of it. We rely on sponsorship, and mongrels are part of the scheme. They're good, intelligent dogs. There's no reason they shouldn't have a purpose in life just like everybody else.'

10
From homes and abroad

Although there are no full-page advertisements in the national press exhorting you to BUY A SECOND-HAND MONGREL, letters from hundreds of satisfied customers like the ones I've seen do give some idea of the advantages. This chapter is given over to just a few of the more amusing and moving testimonials I came across while writing this book. Completely honest about the difficulties, they nevertheless show better than any amount of words from me what a difference a True Dog makes to people's lives. Why pay more?

From journalist Ian Smith, a letter about Samantha (Sam for short), the notorious Duck Dog:

We got her from Lancashire RSPCA kennels when she was about seven months old. She is a very affectionate and lively labrador/ terrier cross who, according to the kennels staff, was the victim of a marriage break-up. It seems the couple concerned were able to compromise about who should get what as far as possessions were concerned – but could not agree who should get custody of the dog! The upshot was that neither should have her and that's how we came to find her looking very sad, forlorn and lost at the kennels. My wife, two sons and two daughters actually went to choose a pet while I was working, and when they came back with Sam, they explained it was because of her looks – and apparent docility – that they selected her. That docility disappeared the second she realized she had found a new home, and within a very few hours she had very firmly established herself in the home . . . and the cat's basket which she tried to claim as her own.

We first learned of her penchant for swimming when the whole family went for a balmy summer's walk in Styal Park, a National Trust property in Cheshire, about a month after Sam came to us. We were at the far end where a river joins the park and runs for about one-and-a-half miles downstream until it reaches a weir. Below the weir it is funnelled into a narrow channel and used to drive the water wheel for a century-old mill about a hundred yards down.

A sudden splash and a shout from Katy, my thirteen-year-old daughter, warned us that Sam was in the water. She was only a few yards from the bank, quite a steep one, and we all rushed to the edge to help her out again. But instead of swimming towards us, she began swimming to the far bank. Foolishly we put this down to panic on her part and all started to scramble for ways to get across the river and rescue her. She was obviously able to swim, did it quite well in fact, but confirmed (or so we thought) that she was in trouble by emitting a continual high-pitched yelp, the sort dogs make when they are hurt or frightened.

The yelping suddenly stopped when she reached a sandbank in the middle of the river. She stood on the bank for a few moments catching her breath, barked, wagged her tail and then dived into the water again. Sam's first training session for the cross-Channel attempt had begun! However hard we shouted, however much we pleaded, she refused even to acknowledge our presence, so intent was she on negotiating her way along the winding river. A few times she came close in to shore but as soon as she realized she was getting dangerously close to arm's-length she veered off towards the middle again – always making this high-pitched yelping noise in between swallowing mouthfuls of water and joyfully spurting them out again like some crazy whale. Two lads, aged about eleven or twelve, were in swimming trunks paddling in one stretch of the water and volunteered to get her out. They swam towards her but hastily turned tail when they got within a few feet and Sam started barking at them. She was obviously determined *no one* was going to spoil her fun.

Eventually we reached the weir with Sam approaching us in the middle of the river about 30 yards behind. My wife Elizabeth shouted that the 'poor thing' was going to get swept over the weir as the river at this point ran fast and furious. Nonsense, I scoffed – if she's strong enough to swim a mile and a half, she's strong enough to paddle over to the bank where we were waiting. She went to the bank all right; trouble was it was on the side furthest away from us. She trod water there for about two minutes, ears pricked up and head turning constantly towards the weir and the sound of rushing water. She obviously thought it too alluring a mystery to ignore and, to our shrieks of discouragement, left the safety of the bank and actually swam to the edge of the 25-foot weir. She managed to clamber on to the stone lip of the weir and stood there looking down, her tail wagging furiously. Then with an excited bark and a final wag of her tail, the lunatic actually launched herself off the weir and into the water pounding down into the narrow channel about 25 feet below.

She must be dead; we were all convinced of it. No one, but no one could have survived that fall. Katy and sister Anna, aged eleven, started crying, the boys were biting back tears, Liz was sobbing and wading to the edge of the weir at the same time and I was racing downstream to get across to the other side where the river passed through a narrow iron grill . . . and where I was sure I would recover the battered body of our pet. But there was no sign of her. I began scouring every bit of water as I moved slowly along the river bank thinking her body must have been carried down to the riverbed. But I couldn't spot it. After about ten minutes, I was in sight of the weir and looked up to see Liz gesturing frantically at me. I couldn't hear what she was saying so broke into a sprint to reach her. As I did so I could see something rust-coloured poking out between this torrent of water racing down the weir face.

It was Sam's tail. She had dived off the weir – now she was climbing back up it again, her paws gripping the few-inches-wide steps running up the almost sheer face. She actually made it . . . I doubt I ever could have. And when she reached the top, she was about to turn round and launch herself off again when Liz lunged out and managed to grab her collar.

Sam had earned her swimming blue. From then on her flirtation with water became a full-blown romance that continues to this day.

She has plunged into the canal and navigated her way between the barges and small boats all coming near to colliding in their frantic efforts to avoid her. She has swum a fair length of the Norfolk Broads when we were daft enough to take her on our boating holiday last year. She has even provided bank holiday drama for families enjoying a quiet day at Lyme Park, near Stockport, Greater Manchester. I foolishly parked our car about a hundred yards from the lake in the centre of this park where about 200 people sat on the edges chatting and eating their picnic teas. When the rear car door opened, Sam shot out, gave a yelp of joy and sprinted for the water. In she went . . . and immediately started the awful yelping. Everyone was convinced she was in trouble. The crowds grew, dozens and dozens of people were encouraging her back to the side. I slinked off and sat in the car. It was too embarrassing to watch.

But after about forty minutes I shamefacedly had to admit ownership. It was either that or watch two security men swim in to rescue this mongrel dog. They had been called by some of the onlookers and begged to save the poor drowning dog who couldn't make her way back to the bank. When I saw one of the security guards stripping to his underpants and the other calling for help in his walkie-talkie handset I had to shuffle up and mutter that it was *my* dog that was causing the panic. The security men weren't pleased; I started getting very dirty looks from some of the crowd, heard several remarks about 'owners who don't care what happens to their poor pets' and tried to ignore the yelps that Sam was still making as she swam round in circles, trying to ingratiate herself with the ducks, doing a bit of trick underwater swimming and generally enjoying herself – disdainfully ignoring the furore going on all around her.

She eventually tired of the water, swam to the bank and hauled herself out, trotting towards me with wagging tail and bright, happy brown eyes.

The incident in Dunham Park, Cheshire, you might already know about from the *Daily Mail* report. We took her with us to the local National Trust park and we weren't quick enough getting her on the leash. There was a splash. There she was, chasing the ducks – well, she didn't exactly chase them – *joining* the ducks, but of course the ducks found it rather strange to see one of their number a thrashing biscuit-coloured creature, and they tried to swim away. There was a crowd forming, small by Sam's standards, so we just sat down and had a smoke, knowing what to expect and that it would be quite pointless calling to her or trying to entice her with sticks, etc. After about twenty-five minutes of high-pitched yelping and sploshing, we heard a much louder splash. Here was a guy in a T-shirt and underpants swimming out towards Sam. My wife shouted, 'It's OK! She's OK!' 'She's in trouble,' shouted the chap, 'I can tell.' 'No, she's OK,' we called, 'really.' 'People like you shouldn't be allowed to have dogs,' bellowed the lifesaver, and he held out his arms towards Sam in a rescuing gesture.

Now, Sam was treading water, doggie-paddling and yelping quietly, and when he held out his hands, she thought this must be a playmate, a fellow water nymph, and started to swim towards him. We were watching all this from the bank and thinking, 'Sam, don't let him catch you.' Well, he got within ten yards of her and it suddenly occurred to Sam that here was somebody about to drag her ashore, so she turned tail and swam off, and as she was twice as strong a swimmer as her rescuer, she soon put some distance between them. He came to the bank eventually, and I felt quite sorry for him because he was with three girls, and here he was, wading out in a sopping T-shirt and seaweed underpants, so when he got out, I went over and quietly explained Sam's previous convictions and thanked him very much. She came ashore of her own accord after an hour-and-a-quarter. We are totally embarrassed by it.

From Brighton RSPCA treasurer, Philip Hale, the story of Adi:

I was driving along Bexhill Road in Eastbourne one morning, and saw this little six-month-old puppy wandering about in the road among the traffic. So I stopped and had a look at the dog. She had a disc on, with her name and address – 'Snuff' something-or-the-other, Bexhill Road – so I took her to the house and nobody was in. It was a very tatty, scruffy, run-down house and while I was knocking at the door, the people from next-door came out and said, 'Oh, have you brought that dog back again? It's always out; they keep it outside all day long and it gets away a lot. They don't seem to care about it. The best thing would be if somebody would come and take it away.' So after making further inquiries I took the dog along to the RSPCA in Brighton. Well, it was about a fortnight later that she found a home in Worthing with a middle-aged couple, and I did an after-visit to see how they were getting on. When I went round there, she'd disappeared. 'She's run off,' they said. 'She keeps running off.' Usually she was chained up outside – they said she was dirty, but because she was quite a nice dog, they'd keep her anyway. A fortnight later, though, she was back at the RSPCA: she was 'dirty' and 'kept running off'. So that was the end of that home.

Now here she was at the kennels, with big ears and nothing special about her, and things were getting a bit desperate because we were very overcrowded at the time and her appointment for the chop was looming large. So I started asking around among my family and friends, as she seemed such a likeable dog, beautiful nature, friendly, interested, affectionate – perfect really. Eventually I found somebody to take her, and they promised me they'd have her neutered. Six months later, they'd let her out on her own, and she was pregnant, even though they'd promised to have her 'done', and she'd had four puppies. They got rid of three of them to homes, and kept one, and the next thing I knew, they wanted to get rid of the mother – she was called 'Lady' now, as opposed to Snuff. So they brought her back to the RSPCA and then that was really going to be it. She'd had three homes, and now she was for the chop. This was a classic case of a dog getting a bad name, because you have to tell a prospective owner the dog's reputation, deserved or not, and if they like, they can use this as an excuse to bring it back when they're fed up with it.

So I said to a friend of mine, Pauline, 'Look, I'm very fond of this dog; unless we do something, she's going to be put down.' So she said, 'OK, I'll keep her until you can find her a home.' She has been with Pauline ever since. True, she peed on the carpet once, and got a smack, and that was the end of it. She isn't 'dirty indoors', and she has never, ever disappeared, or run off. Never ever. Look at her. You couldn't ask for a nicer dog. Nobody wanted her because she's a bit silly-looking with those big ears she's got, and a bit of a scruff-bag. People want a dog they can be proud to be seen with, I

suppose. You wouldn't be proud of her, would you? Well, I would
as well, but then we're not typical.

From Jenny Kearney, owner of East Lodge Grooming in Worthing, about Beanie and Rats:

I think Ratty could enter any of the classes at Scruffts. He had a
bath last night, he was so rotten. He ate some cooking oil – not just
some. You'd think that after a bottle of it he'd have been sick or had
the runs. They were both perfectly all right. Beanie's still got oil on
his head, but they've got strong stomachs. Rats has got the
scavenger instinct still. He will pick up anything – bath crystals,
soap, talcum powder, lumps of concrete and worse. I think it's
because he had to scavenge to survive. He once knocked down a
paint pot with brushes in it and one paintbrush was never
found.

Rats, the blond one, was found on a rubbish tip. Beanie's very
afraid of men, but Rats loves everybody. Carol here found Rattie
on the tip with a gash round his neck, and he needed five stitches,
and Beanie was found two or three months later lying in the gutter.
If only we knew what happened to him. When we first brought him
in here, he wouldn't stand, he wouldn't walk. Carol took him to the
Blue Cross because she thought perhaps every bone in his body
was broken; they kept him in overnight and said there was nothing
physically wrong with him, but that he wouldn't walk and he was in
a state of shock. The nurse said, 'You may get him to walk, you may
not, or he may decide one day to just *bolt* – it's up to you.' So we
brought him back and put him on the floor and he just sat there –
all day. He didn't move, and his huge eyes followed you around,
and nothing you could do would make him relax. We had to carry
him to the car and put him in it, carry him back, put him on the
floor – about three days of this, and then he stood up. Finally he
stood. And then gradually he would start walking around in here.
By this time, Rats was living in this towel cabinet: it was winter, and
it was cosy, and he took this over – this was his house. We had to
take all the towels out, and Beanie wanted to be in there, so they
shared the house, and Beanie got quite brave. During the day his
little tail would wag and he'd hop in and out, but as soon as the
collars and leads were brought out for going home, Beanie would
start to shake. It meant the Great Outside again.

After about a week, we said, 'Well, this is ridiculous. He *can* walk
– we can't keep carrying him everywhere.' So we left the door open
and we all took Rats and Sam, my collie, and we said goodbye,
we're going – and walked off without him. You could see by his face
that he was having an internal battle with himself – 'I want to go
with them but I can't' – and at last he won, and he followed us, very
slowly at first and then running up the road behind us, and that

was it. He was fine. *Now* when you get the collars and leads, he jumps up and down, grabs Rats' lead – it's mayhem. Goes to the park, all perfectly normal, at least with people that he knows. We've now got to get him to accept strangers. It makes you wonder what had happened to the little fellow.

Miss F. M. Hill, writing to the NCDL about Violette:

I used to dislike dogs – much preferred cats – so you will be wondering why I am writing telling you that a dog has now become my closest and most beloved friend, and has completely changed my life, for I am an agoraphobic.

Violette is a German shepherd cross whom I rescued from an animal sanctuary and who was – when I brought her home – a shaking, frightened, bewildered dog, who had been badly treated, was terrified of her own shadow, and hated men on sight. Her previous world had been on shifting sand and she had run away and been a stray for several weeks before the sanctuary took her in.

Training was a problem. She hated men, and children too, for they had teased her unmercifully, and my hopes of her being 'normal' were rather quickly dashed. I then heard of a man who specialized in 'difficult' dogs, and through his teaching I have been able to turn Violette into my constant companion and I can now go out of the house to the parks, and walk around my own area which had been a nightmare before and forced me to stay indoors even when it was a glorious day and I needed to get out.

Unless you have agoraphobia, you will be quite unable to understand what a complete hell it is. At times, I have been unable to get out of my chair, feeling as if I had been chained to it, when all I wanted to do was go into the kitchen for a cup of tea. Violette has changed all that. We almost read each other's thoughts – and if I want to go out I no longer go alone. We're both female, we've both suffered, but together we can face the world.

If any agoraphobic reads this, I beg you to get a dog – you will have unquestioning love and support and a friend who will never let you down. Take your courage in both hands and go out – I did – and life is good, and worth living again.

From Linda Humphreys of Tring, on her Kahla:

Kahla is now well settled having been with me for just over a year. The change in her personality has been very significant. She is no longer timid and so nervous. She is much more relaxed. Whatever has happened to her in the past has not altered her wonderfully gentle nature and fierce loyalty to those who have grown to love her. I do not consider myself to be her 'owner' – she is my friend.

My three cats allow themselves to be washed by her and rub their faces up and down her long snout. Kahla had been in rescue kennels for a long time. This was due to the fact that most people when looking for a dog prefer a pretty dog or a puppy. As she does not come into either of these categories, she was overlooked for five months, until my friend Pip visited the kennels and returned with her.

I refute all statements about mongrels not being loyal or easy to handle – Kahla has been more than easy to handle; I have not had to 'teach' her to behave and she has always had respect for my home and for my friends.

If I have been feeling unwell, it is she that comforts me. Although she is about eight years old, when she goes out she is just like a puppy.

It would break my heart to be parted from her now. But if I did have to go away, I could think of dozens of people who would be only too delighted to give her a home.

Kahla is the second rescue dog I've had. They make better companions – I won't say 'pets' because I don't like the word. She is very protective towards me, and incredible with children. People say, when we go visiting, 'Where's Kahla?' if we don't bring her – she's terribly popular. There are a few things that make her frightened enough to shake all over, as though she has been hit. She's frightened of bicycles – not of motorbikes or cars, just bicycles. I didn't rough-and-tumble with her at home for a long time, because I didn't know how she'd react – she had obviously been beaten because she was quite scarred – but she's grown a lot younger since we've had her. She can't swim, but she plays cricket and hockey with the children and pinches their shoes.

From the former Secretary of the National Anti-Vivisection Society, Brian Gunn, concerning Jason:

I've been in vivisection laboratories throughout the world, from America to Scandinavia, to Mexico, Spain, China and Japan as well as in England, and when I think of all the laboratories I've visited, the Japanese must be the top of the cruelty table. It seems there is no compassion at all for animals in that country and this applies not only to laboratory animals but to the pets they keep in their homes. I bought, in a pet shop in Japan, a dog collar, widely on sale, only it's a dog collar with a difference. There are prongs sticking out at the back and the prongs are electrodes, powered by a 9–volt battery. When the dog barks, the electrodes, embedded in the dog's neck, give it an electric shock. I've had the collar tested in an electronics laboratory back in Britain, and I'm informed that whereas the voltage from a mains electric supply is 240 volts, the voltage from this collar when a dog barks is 350 volts; in other words, it's a lot stronger than actually plugging the dog into a household socket. As a result, the dogs have fits, and if a dog happened to be standing in a wet area when it barked, it would probably be electrocuted. Cooked alive. Now, this is a device widely available in Japan, and gives some indication what the Japanese are routinely doing to their so-called pets, animals they 'love'. So I think you can well imagine the animal suffering that I witnessed and photographed in Japanese vivisection laboratories. It was like entering the Gates of Hell.

Now, I had a press photograph taken of a dog back in Britain wearing the Japanese collar, with the 9-volt battery removed of course, to show what it looks like. I'm glad to say that particular dog looks *happy* with it on, because it's my own dog, Jason. Everybody thinks his own dog is the best in the world, and mine is a mongrel, a real Heinz 57, who was obtained from a dogs' home. He'd been very badly treated, and the first few weeks I had him, he cowered if I put my arm down suddenly. He'd obviously been beaten around the head. I took him to the vet straightaway, only to be told that the dog had distemper, and that the best thing to do was to put him down. It was a waste of time and money trying to do anything for him, because he was probably going to die. But Jason fought it. He had a great will and courage to live, though I don't know what he'd been through before. He was found wandering round the streets of Coventry, and for many months afterwards, he used to ravage in the dustbins for food.

Many people have had novel experiences with dogs they've rescued from the dogs' homes, but Jason once got me into a very embarrassing situation indeed, when I thought the ground must definitely open up and swallow me. Central TV wanted to do an interview with me for a programme about vivisection, and they were going to film it by the River Avon, as a nice backdrop. They wanted to know if I had a dog – perhaps to try and make me look a bit normal. I said, yes, I've got a dog, a mongrel. They weren't very impressed. Could he do tricks? I said, well, no, he hasn't actually come out of a circus, so they said, well, perhaps you can throw a stick and he can fetch it back to you. Now, Jason doesn't believe in fetching sticks – he thinks it's silly. So I said no – if I let him off the lead in this park to bring back a stick, it will take me two hours to catch him. Oh well, they said, despairingly, perhaps in that case, you can just *take him for a walk on the lead*, and we'll film you coming towards the camera along the river. Fine. So there we were, in front of the Royal Shakespeare Theatre, right on the edge of the Avon, and a small crowd had gathered to watch the filming. The director said, 'Right. Go fifty yards down there, and when I say

come, you walk towards me naturally with the dog. Right *Come!*'
And Jason lunged, and pulled like hell, and ended up in the river
after some swans and ducks.

From Margaret von Hoensbroech, on the Great Mazinga:

Mazinga is a darling – her name is an anagram of 'amazing'
because that's what she is. You could stick a day-old baby in her
mouth with absolute confidence, though she does tend to nip post
ladies' bottoms. She was found in the remote outskirts of
Dunstable, an area where dogs are frequently dumped, according
to the kennel staff. Mazinga had been abandoned, though she was
lucky – at least it wasn't on a motorway, and she had somewhere to
hide. The vet who examined her said she was in her first season,
when she'd had pups – I reckon this was why they got rid of her.
This was July, holiday time, when they come flooding in at the
kennels, and when people going on holiday make a slight detour in
the car to abandon their dogs. She was very frightened and timid.
She was covered in eczema, had scabby ears and baldy patches
round her eyes. She'd stop as you approached and then run off
when you tried to catch her. It took us several months to rehabilitate her. She was scared of men, feet and sticks, even walking sticks.

But she's terrific now. She has frilly knickers and a feathery tail –
we had no idea she would develop these qualities! She certainly is
an adaptable type of dog but I think this is because I just take her
everywhere with me and take it for granted that she will behave
well. And she does. She's very popular with all my friends and a
great campaigner for animal rights – an excellent flag-seller on all
animal welfare flag days.

Mongrels are wonderful creatures. The ones that have been
treated badly seem to develop into marvellous, loving dogs, all the
more appreciative of their owners and their homes. I enclose a
couple of photos of my dear Mazinga – the 'alert' one is a bit dark
although it's my favourite. She looks like this when I talk to her and
tell her the names of her favourite people, or the word 'biscuit'.
The 'soulful' picture shows her kindness. She's not at all sad, but
always patient. All our cats, kittens, tame rats, hens, rabbits and the
cockatiel have adored her. She used to allow the rabbit to run
under her tummy in the garden.

From Cherry Mitchell of Wood Green Animal Shelter, the tale of Bambi:

Please find enclosed a photo of Bambi, my little black-and-tan
bitch found two years ago living in the back of an old car behind a
petrol station. I was asked by a lady who owns a grocer's shop in
Bishop's Stortford to try and catch a little dog who was 'living

rough' behind the station, and I tracked her down early one morning as she was darting in and out of the traffic on the busy A11, very nearly being killed. I located her 'nest' – a very old Vauxhall with the back door hanging off, and I emptied a tin of meat on to the back seat (which she had torn to shreds to make a bed). After a long wait, she came and jumped into the car, and I slammed the door behind her and managed to get her on a collar and lead. She was one of the most frightened dogs I have ever seen, even working at an animal shelter.

I didn't really have facilities at that time to have another dog, so I took her to the shelter with the hope that someone else might like her. Several people did, but they all brought her back the day after saying she was 'strange' or 'odd', and wouldn't settle. The time came when she should have been put to sleep, but I felt responsible for her so I took her home. Those people who each had her for one night weren't joking when they said she was odd. These are just some of the odd things she does: sits in the kitchen sink, sleeps on tops of wardrobes, cupboards, etc., gets in and out of windows (upstairs included), hides in cupboards or boxes left open, jumps *any* height, sits on tables and windowsills, runs away at the sound of thunder or gunfire (we live in the country), will not stay in any home or anywhere without me being present, runs up and down the stairs sometimes for two to three hours at a time, loves to get in with the puppies at the shelter, carries something in her mouth 90 per cent of the day – and many more strange antics. Her good points are: she loves my other dog Ted, loves me and shows it, is now housetrained, which she wasn't at first, and is just fun to have around. It might be prudent to mention that the first time I took her in my car she chewed every seat to shreds (the old nest-building again?) and I also have receipts, etc. to prove that she has chewed her way through approximately £2000.00 worth of antique furniture I have (or had) in my home. I would be delighted if she were included in your book, not for myself, but because she is such a brave little dog, the like of which I have never seen before nor am likely to see again.

The sterling girls at Battersea not only spend their daylight hours finding homes for thousands of inmates; they rescue some of the saddest and worst cases themselves. Mongrels like Blackie, rejected by half-a-dozen different owners and now resident; Tina, the black-and-tan bitch who came in pregnant and surly; Leila, the cross collie who likes it in surgery; and Nelly, found as a pup hanging in a liftshaft with her dead brothers and sisters. Nelly developed a depressive personality, easily demoralized, especially by the arrival of new dogs more presentable than she, covered in bubble gum and misery. The slightest setback even now throws her into a bad mood: she likes life to be as orderly as possible. She is now bearing up as cheerfully as she can with a kind family in Chislehurst, despite sharing the home with three other dogs. Another staff dog of Battersea, who happens to be my favourite of all the featured waifs, was found very badly injured after a road accident. Already old and grey-whiskered, he was nevertheless patched up and nursed back to health, and renamed after the metal dog in *Battlestar Galactica*. He spent the remaining year of his life in uproarious naughtiness, and the girls loved him so much that they wrote him a little dedication:

DAGGATT

Dark brown eyes going blue,
Worn brown teeth.
Toes and whiskers white with knowledge,
Stiff joints and bad habits
. . . our Daggatt.

Adopting mongrels from the streets and shelters of Britain is one thing; homing them from overseas is quite another because of the UK's stringent anti-rabies quarantine laws. In July 1983, an Irish wolfhound, imported from the United States, died in quarantine in Rugby and, shortly before, a woman from Stroud, returning to Britain from India, died of the disease. Britain continues to fend off an outbreak like the one that occurred here in 1917 by requiring all incoming animals to serve six months at approved kennels, where they may be visited frequently and where they are looked after by sympathetic staff. The Ministry of Agriculture, Fisheries and Food do not approve of rabies vaccination, so as not to build up a 'pool' of vaccinated animals should an outbreak occur, and permission to import a dog must be obtained beforehand from them (*see* Appendix 6). The Ministry will licence a carrier to convey the dog from its port of entry to the quarantine kennels of your choice.

Between 1984 and 1987, 148 people were caught trying to import a dog illegally, any one of which could have caused a rabies catastrophe in this country. It isn't worth it. But it *is* unquestionably worth importing a mongrel from overseas legally and through the proper channels, even for all the money, trouble and red tape involved. Six months passes very quickly for a dog well fed and looked after, compared with the extended misery of a mongrel's life in many lands abroad. The International Fund for Animal Welfare write to me regularly with news of dogs they have saved *en masse* from the cooking pots and markets of the Philippines and South Korea, where mongrels are bound with wire in tiny cages, foaming at the mouth with fear while they wait to have their fur burned off with blow-torches, to be slowly hanged to tenderize their meat. In Peking in 1984, 400,000 dogs were clubbed and drowned and driven into electric fences by order of the charming Chinese government, and in Spain and Greece, hungry mongrels rake over empty crisp packets and tin cans, their souls in their eyes staring at British tourists. A few, very few, strike it lucky.

Zoe, a Greek mongrel with kite-ears and a rounders-bat tail, is worth every penny of the £1200 it cost Angela and Barry Mays to retrieve her from Corfu. The North London couple first spotted her hanging about outside their holiday apartment in Kavos; she had dug a burrow for her five pups in the bole of a tree and, in her dog way, told the Mayses all her troubles. They came home feeling unhappy about the dog, though they had found someone to look after her back in Greece. Zoe's big ears and bravery continued to haunt them, and when they heard that she had gone missing, they determined to go out and rescue her and bring her back to Britain. They couldn't find her. Angela Mays walked for miles calling for 'Zoe!' and crying every time she saw a chocolate-coloured mongrel who wasn't her. Eventually after one wild goose chase and with the help of a newspaper and Sunmed Holidays, Mr Mays went out again to Corfu and there, outside the apartment where they had first seen her, was their jewel, ravaging in the rubbish. She has now served her six months in quarantine and will never be parted from the Mayses again. 'A lot of people have said we are mad, especially for spending all the money. I can't really explain why we have done it,' says Mrs Mays, 'except to say that we love her.'[1]

The Rossiter family met a friend while they were on holiday in Spain – elegant Bella, proud mother of eight, all huddled in a drain in Alicante. Bella's scruffy yet refined features so endeared her to the Rossiters that, when they drove away leaving her in a makeshift sanctuary, they made up their minds, no matter how absurd and difficult it was, to bring her home to their house at Hook, Hampshire. After a lot of bureaucracy and six months at finishing school, Bella is now merrily digging holes in the Rossiter garden. It took nine months altogether and nearly £1000, but as engineer Tony Rossiter says, 'It has been worth every penny if you consider the state she was in before. She is very boisterous and seems to be making up for her lost childhood.'[2]

Why do these people do it? I've never seen it summed up better than in Shakespeare's Sonnet XXIX, the one that ends:

> . . . *For thy sweet love remember'd such wealth brings*
> *That then I scorn to change my state with kings.*

11

Mongrel leisure

A bored dog is an unhappy dog, and play is as necessary to mongrels as to people. This is why they will accost us with balls and slippers, planting them just out of reach to tantalize us and performing the traditional dog 'play bow' with their 'elbows' resting on the floor. Puppies play at rough-and-tumble and gnaw-your-face-off to learn the hunting skills of their ancestors, and adult dogs play for the same reason we do – they need to be revitalized by the magic of games. Mock-fighting is a great favourite, provided tempers do not flare. *Do* be careful with a newly acquired rescue dog, and see that mutual respect is observed. If you think the dog is getting upset, call a time-out immediately, and never overtire a pup or an elderly dog. Dogs wishing to 'pretend fight' with a physical inferior will lie on the ground with ears and tail signalling 'animated', hoping by this submissive behaviour to get the little runt interested in a set-to. Mongrels will also pounce on their belongings, roll over and hold a toy in the air with their forepaws, pretending to be attacked by it.

Ball games are also excellent fun, and good exercise, although mongrels are not natural retrievers and may be inclined to take the ball and disappear over the horizon, or throw it down at the first distraction and forget where they've put it. Large, *visible*-size balls and beach balls are, in any case, preferable: I have already mentioned the case of a police dog with a tennis ball lodged in his throat like a gob-stopper. Sticks are fun, too, but beware of sharp wedges and splinters; choose a big, solid round one. Dogs will play hide-and-seek, tug-of-war and chase-me with exactly the same enthusiasm as children, and large dogs love to get humans on the ground and sit on them if at all possible.

Like Edward VII's Caesar, whose hobbies were listed as 'hunting and motoring', intelligent dogs have exotic tastes. Boating, riding on motorbikes, making serious collections of old kettles and pieces of flint, and even tapping out morse-code messages like the famous 'talking dogs' of Germany – you'd be surprised what dogs get up to during their tea breaks. One of the most amusing things I've ever heard was a mongrel trio singing to the music of a piano accordion in Small Heath, Birmingham. Their owner, Irish inventor Mr Leo Donnellan, is actually a mongrel breeder and keeps photographs of the present generation's mother and grandmother about the house, lovingly framed. Paddy, Charlie and Sally, the canine equivalent of the Bachelors, have their own hand-crafted half-inch-plywood units on furniture castors, which can be hung with curtains for privacy or hooked up to the back of Mr Donellan's bicycle and driven for twenty miles to see the sights.

I was treated to a medley of the trio's greatest hits, a quite unforgettable experience. The dogs look forward to a recital and become very excited when the accordion appears. Paddy squeals movingly, being the prima donna and most melodic of the three. 'They have to shout for a time while I'm tuning up,' says Mr Donnellan. 'It takes a while.' Suddenly though, at the opening bars of 'Oh Danny Boy', the trio issue from their bed units, raise their noses ceilingwards and let out a plaintive and quite ear-splitting rendition of the popular Irish number, with Charlie and Sally barking a discordant base and Paddy handling the high notes. 'Bless This House', followed by 'Auld Lang Syne', followed by 'The Minstrel Boy' deafen the inhabitants of Oldknow Road with a quite thrilling cacophony. These aren't exceptional mongrels, according to their accompanist. 'They're not particularly clever dogs; it's just fascinating to know the interest they can have in things. Once I had nine pups here, and, with the two dogs, that was eleven. I'd give them all individual treatment, so they got to know their names. A dog should be taught to use its brain, and all you have to do to train a dog is to be schooled yourself, and school the dog in the same way. If somebody had told you "yes" was "no" and "no" was "yes", you'd be in a mess, wouldn't you? You should never ever hit a dog, though I do a bit of shouting.' Sally, Charlie and Paddy are all from the one litter – 'Charlie and Sally look a bit the same all right, but Paddy is short-haired, like his mother.'

We are interrupted in these considerations by Sally fetching her shopping basket from the kitchen. 'The first trailer I made for the bicycle, Sally wouldn't get in it. She was worried about carrying her basket.' Sally looks ruefully round the room at Mr Donnellan's inventions, Heath Robinson mobiles on magnetic tops, layers of spinning 78 rpm records and whirling-dervish figures in perpetual motion. 'I'm not an inventor; I'm a discoverer. Who knows; maybe I pick up the ideas from the dogs, rather like a radio receiver.' Inspired by the mongrel? 'I don't like the term "mongrel" at all. Who's to say what crosses there were in the beginning, before breeds were made?' Who indeed, though the neighbours of Oldknow Road no doubt think they have their crosses to bear.

Immortality, like fame, tends not to come the way of even the most talented and vivacious mongrel dog. This is why devoted owners have albums full of snaps of their pets fishing, begging, sitting on cliffs and rummaging in rabbit holes. You need a decent camera because dogs are inveterate fidgets and a pose once lost is gone for ever. Paw prints are a popular doggie memento: you can do one yourself for your dog by dipping his paw gently in watercolour, splodging it on to paper and framing it when dry, though do remember to wash the paint off the paw, or you'll have prints all over the house. Plaster of Paris prints are even more effective, and make nice Christmas gifts to fellow dog lovers; or for the really special occasion, there's the personal dog portrait, capturing your mongrel on canvas, the standard of commercial dog portraiture being very high.

Apart from professional dog photographers – consult the dog press or your Yellow Pages for contacts – there are a number of extremely good painters specializing in dogs. The Cadogan Gallery in London have an annual exhibition of dog portraits, and a recent very fine display of the work of Michelle

Pearson Cooper gave some idea of the talent materializing in the field. There is nothing sentimental or soppy about a Pearson Cooper dog portrait. Say the gallery, 'She studies the animal's movements, whether walking, sitting or playing, and can create three or four of these different poses as well as the conventional Victorian single portrait.' Crufts Best-in-Show portraitist, Julie Brenan, works from sketches and studies she makes of the dog herself, and these are tirelessly built up into a likeness on canvas, developing from the skeleton outwards. When she reaches an impasse, she does what Vincent Van Gogh used to do and turns the painting upside down to get a fresh view.

I had my own mongrel Stanley immortalized by another quite brilliant animal artist, an oil painter and watercolourist in the West Midlands, Nigel Hemming, whose work I first spotted in the Halcyon Gallery in Birmingham Shopping Centre. (He works from home, *see* Appendix 6 for address.) Nigel's dog portraits look more like the dogs than their photographs – irrefutably accurate and a delight to study. Says Nigel, 'Anyone can take a photograph. There are very few households that don't own a camera, and if they've got a dog, ten to one they'll have photographs of it. But to have an original painting is totally different. OK, a photo and a painting are both two-dimensional facsimiles, but when you take a photograph, you capture only a fraction of time. No matter how much preparation you put into creating it, you still have absolutely no control over the conditions of that image in the fraction of a second that the shutter is open. With a painting, you're in total control from the first brush-stroke to the last. It's totally labour intensive.' What is the artist looking for? 'Character. Every dog is an individual, with its own personality and it own posture characteristics. It isn't enough to just get the spots right on a dalmatian.' Nigel doesn't much care for the 'court portraiture' of show dogs. 'They've got to be in the classic show pose – four square, head out, tail out. Boring,' he says, which is why he prefers to cater for the pet portrait market, providing a sort of service to dog-loving owners. 'I really cater for Joe Public, rather than professional show people. There are very few professionals seriously aiming at the market I'm in.'

Why doesn't he concentrate on pedigrees, like so many dog painters? 'You'd be surprised how many mongrel pictures I do. One of the best portraits I ever painted was a mongrel. As far as I allow myself to be satisfied, I was with that one – a cracker of a mongrel bitch called Katie. Mongrels are very individual.' (His portrait of Stanley appears in the last photograph section.) He works from photographs, which he prefers wherever possible to take himself, so that he can study the dog and capture its character in a pose. 'You will get purists who say, "Oh, I never use photographs." Well, I could say a rude word about that. The important thing is to give satisfaction to the customer, and that is my goal. Photographs are the easiest way of getting a picture done. I used to draw from life when I first started, and for me it was a total waste of time. I only met one dog that would sit long enough for me to get a few marks on the paper, and that was a little old mongrel who would sit for hours if you put a button on his paw. I couldn't bear to see him sitting there looking at me. They don't sit usually. They fidget about, except when they're asleep, and nobody wants a portrait of a dog lying asleep. You want something alive.'

Nigel is primarily a watercolourist, although he does work in oils if requested. He feels that watercolour is *the* animal medium because it is so spontaneous and permits so much scope for detail – naturalistic detail is his speciality. He does landscapes, people, a few cats 'and I've done horses', but dogs are his bread-and-butter as a professional artist, working nine or ten hours a day ('I can usually, flat out, get one picture done in a day') and on a price-to-size basis. 'I must be perfectly honest with you: I'm not a dog nut. We have a dog in the house which is my wife's rather than mine, which doesn't mean I don't like dogs – I do – but what I really like is working with them and painting them.' Most of his commissions are personal presents from husbands to wives and *vice versa*. 'It's quite funny actually because I often have to sneak round with my camera taking photographs when the husband is out. I don't know what the neighbours must think! But a portrait of a dog is very enduring, as a one-off. Dogs become part of the family, and when they're gone, there's nothing that can bring them back, but to have a portrait of them to keep for ever is a little bit special. It's a way of remembering them, of showing that you care for them.'

Whether your mongrel wants his portrait done, or his paw printed, or just a big marrowbone gift-wrapped in a shoebox, the gift most mongrels appreciate *most* is a holiday with you. Holidays abroad are not possible for dogs because the homeward trip would be complicated by six months in quarantine. If you *must* go abroad, you should book your mongrel into kennels *when you book your holiday*. If you leave it until the last minute, all available spaces will be taken. Year after year, the dogs' homes are littered with canine 'vacation tragedies' and for many a mongrel, holidays are the saddest days of their lives. Visit the kennels of your choice and ask to be shown around. Staff should be friendly and co-operative, and kennels should be clean, with raised sleeping berths and good exercise areas. Otherwise, go somewhere else, for goodness sake. No reputable kennels will take any dog without an up-to-date vaccination record and, while you're at it, you should also ask about kennel cough vaccine.

If you feel unhappy about kennelling your loving mongrel while you're off enjoying yourself – and, as Jilly Cooper has pointed out, rescue mongrels may become quite demented at being placed in what they take to be another canine doss-house – you should either leave the poor little devil with a reliable friend while you're away, or alter your holiday retreat. You can take a dog from Britain to the Isle of Man, the Channel Isles, Northern Ireland or Eire without quarantine restrictions, and you can take him all over Britain to the most delightful land and seascapes imaginable, provided you check the hotel accommodation beforehand. The RAC Yearbook contains information on dog-guest prices and prohibitions, or you can use what I use – *Pets Welcome*, an annual holiday handbook for dog owners, complete with maps, for 95p (1984 edition), established as *the* rule-of-thumb guide by Herald Handbooks. It gives details of friendly, dogs-welcome accommodation of every type throughout Britain, supported by editorial comment on where to go and where to stay. Over 2500 dog-in holiday opportunities are provided, as well as a section on selected boarding kennels and catteries. *Pets Welcome* is on sale at bookshops and newsagents or obtainable from Herald Holiday Handbooks (*see* Appendix 6 for address), though they tend to sell out if you leave it late in the year.

There is only one teensie problem about coastal holiday arrangements – check for possible beach bans. Squalid little local authorities like Torbay in Devon and Bournemouth, forgetting the tide of human sewage washing in and out on Britain's coastline, have recently taken it upon themselves to ban dogs from their pathetic beaches. Certain other cranky West Country coastal local councils may also impose restrictions. Ask before you go; it would serve them right if you were to go somewhere else. Fortunately these miseries are in the minority: most resorts welcome dogs. PR officer of the NCDL, Clarissa Baldwin: 'We've got one particular member who runs a hotel in Southbourne and she will only *take* people who go on holiday with their dogs!' Thank heaven for the sane, and for the heartening sight of Her Majesty the Queen in her headscarf, sporting with her little dogs on the Norfolk coast. A dog has as much right to see the sea as the next sailor.

12
The vale of years

Nothing binds dogs and humans like their mortality. Faithfulness unto death is taken for granted in the dog, and only the most extraordinary cases achieve public acclaim – the case of Greyfriars Bobby, who outlived his Midlothian farmer master by fourteen years yet would not leave his grave, surviving on buns from Traill's restaurant in Edinburgh; the case of Fido, the rheumatic mutt decorated by the Italian government for his thousands of journeys to the bus-stop where his dead master used to arrive home from work. There have been the dogs found by rescue teams on mountains and moorlands guarding the long-dead remains of walkers and shepherds, and dogs accompanying their owners to the cell and the scaffold. One of Sir Edwin Landseer's most famous paintings, the *Old Shepherd's Chief Mourner*, a collie with his chin resting pathetically on his master's coffin, is true to life in every detail – dog grief over humans knows no decent bounds. The mongrel thinks no less of us when we grow old and incapable, which is why elderly people have a responsibility to find someone else to exercise their dogs when they cannot do it themselves, and pensioners of both species deserve special consideration for their frailty and wisdom. The NCDL have sponsored blocks for their ancient dogs.

A mongrel's life expectancy is longer than that of most pedigrees: around fourteen years is about average, with little terrierish types surviving longer than large types and giant crossbreeds. It isn't really true that one human year is equivalent to seven dog years; as vet David Taylor points out in his book,[1] a much better conversion table was worked out by the French veterinarian Dr Lebeau, who said the first dog year was equal to about fifteen human years, the second dog year to about nine more, and subsequent years of the dog's age equivalent to about four human years each. By this reckoning, a three-year-old dog would be twenty-eight, and a 15-year-old, about seventy-six. The record for longevity is at present held by a 27¼-year-old pedigree, a Lincolnshire labrador, though there are many unsubstantiated mongrel challengers, and Jilly Cooper's book includes a 21½-year-old called Peter Ferris among its venerable ones. Old age in dogs seldom lasts more than a couple of years, during which time they most appreciate the routines they have always been used to and don't like to be traumatized by change or upheaval.

Causes of death in dogs are rather different from the causes of human fatalities. Although they share with us the same degenerative disorders of the heart, kidneys, circulation and faculties, and although dogs suffer from cancers both benign and malignant, the actual cause of death is frequently 'unnatural' – they often die as a result of accidents or euthanasia, i.e. 'mercy-killing'. The ageing dog is more vulnerable to accident and disease because he gradually loses everything needful for his survival and self-esteem – his muscle-tone, hearing, eyesight, pigmentation, stamina, waistline, teeth, handsomeness, metabolic efficiency, appetite, taste, smell and alertness of mind. He can't any longer be bothered to do his bally bottom button up.

COAT An ageing dog's coat tends to become coarse and requires thorough grooming to keep it from getting scurfy and smelly. Bathing with a suitable shampoo obtainable from your vet, provided you keep the dog warm, will make him feel nice and fresh again. Rub him down afterwards with a rough towel, and make sure you also do this when he comes in from the rain. If he shivers a lot in general, he may be grateful for an overcoat or knitted woolly for outdoors. Dogs go grey for the same reason as humans – an inefficiency in the ability to synthesize the pigment melanin – so don't be surprised if he gradually acquires white eyebrows, white muzzle or even a polar-bear skin all over.

DEMANDS   Old dogs tend to be a bit grumpy, a bit sorry for themselves. They raise the pitch of their voices, demanding attention to their needs because they feel wretched and helpless. Please be patient; a dog's old age is very brief compared with ours, and the inconvenience will not last long.

DIET   An old dog may need less food. His metabolism slows down and he can't exercise with the same vigour as a young dog, so many mutts get fat. But frequently an old dog will eat voraciously and lose weight since absorption becomes less efficient. He needs less protein, but what he has should be of high quality. Replace some of his meat with milk or egg. Vitamin supplements may be recommended by a vet, especially the B vitamins, though cheese and beef extract will cheer up tiring tastebuds and provide excellent nutrients. Offal may cause flatulence. There are several excellent ready-made diets for ailing and convalescent dogs – your vet will be glad to give you details. Tinned food may be more convenient for the elderly dog because it slides down easily. Put the dish on a raised surface if it hurts your dog to bend down. Many dogs that 'lose their appetites' are simply stiff and sore. Two or three smaller meals are better for an old digestive system than one large one – remember that senility is a little like puppyhood and you won't go far wrong. If you have a skinny old dog, rather than a fat one, consult the vet. This may be a sign of a specific degenerative disease.

EARS   Deafness in a mongrel is often mistaken by the owner for insolence or stubbornness. Clap your hands behind the dog's head; if he doesn't blink or turn round, he may well be hard of hearing. If this is the case, have more patience, not less. Deafness is quite common in old dog pensioners and remedies are mostly of the palliative sort. Don't let him get lost, don't be impatient with him, but apart from the obvious nuisance to you, he can manage very well.

EYES   Degenerative diseases of the eye are common in dogs, and blindness is something they seem to be able to adapt to very well, relying on smell to a large extent., Provided you don't shift the furniture about too much, a dog can live quite happily without being able to see, though always stay with him in unfamiliar terrain and don't let him out in a driveway or near traffic without his lead on. A condition called *nuclear sclerosis*, in which the lens becomes more dense, is very common and will not usually impair the dog's sight: its presence is discernible in a whitish or bluish haze on the lens in the region of the pupil. Cataracts are more of a hindrance but less common; they are not usually removed in dogs, partly because elderly animals do not respond well to the trauma of surgery.

HEART DISEASE Obesity is often a contributing factor. Consult the vet, who will recommend a special diet, and keep to it assiduously. The reduction of salt in the diet sometimes helps enormously. Advances in veterinary medicine in recent years have run parallel to the human field and there are many research programmes in the offing to do with pacemakers and surgical by-passes.

JOINTS Arthritis is common in elderly canines. Lameness tends to be more of a problem for the dog when he first gets up, and is oiled away by a little exercise – 'little and often' is the key for ageing dog routines. Aspirin may be given as an interim measure, but always consult the vet if you have a creaky dog because there are other remedies. Keep the animal warm and dry, and if you can afford to buy him a new bed, a beanbag or sagbag will help him get up from a recumbent position much more easily. Being overweight tends to make matters worse, so watch your pet's waistline.

KIDNEYS Kidney dysfunction seems to afflict dogs particularly in old age, and may cause the dog to drink more and consequently urinate more. Don't be cross – he can't help it. Bedwetting and housewetting that occur as the result of disease should never be punished. Revert to puppy routines and take the dog outside periodically whether he asks to go or not. Polyester-fur bed linings can be easily washed, and the dog will be very grateful for a little extra help with his hygiene.

Don't stint on the water, but if he really guzzles, try to ration it to 'little and often'.

NAILS   Toenails grow mandarin-like from not being worn away by vigorous running. Keep them short and comfortable.

TEETH   Yellowing and tartar on the teeth can be removed by a vet, and this scaling will also help with the problem of pongy breath. Don't bother with deodorant pills – they're silly. If necessary, a dog can have all his teeth removed without affecting his ability to eat – they don't chew their food anyway – so don't worry about dentures for dogs. Many a human grandfather can crack nuts with his hard gums.

TUMOURS   Warts and little cauliflower-like growths are not uncommon and probably quite harmless. Malignant tumours are a matter for the vet. Surgery and radiation therapy are not always the kindest course for an elderly dog, even though they may prolong his life for a little while. Try to look at it from the dog's point of view and consider what is to be gained by the distress of hospitalization and gruelling treatment programmes. A dog is entitled to dignity first and sentimentality second. It is a matter of close liaison with your vet.

Although the physical problems of senility and old age may persist for a year or so, most dogs unfortunately do not die in their sleep. They die in the sleep we give them, if we have any heart at all. It is up to you as a loving owner to decide when you think life has become a burden rather than a pleasure for your dog; remember that, in the wild, he would not linger long, and only human intervention has prolonged his life into this twilight. If the animal is in incurable pain or distress, incontinent, uncomfortable and miserable, please talk to your regular vet about a dignified end. To drag a dog's life on into the mist of vacancy and pain is not a kindness to him; it is only a means of avoiding your responsibility.

Veterinary surgeon Tony Cowie has definite opinions on the

subject: 'You always know when the time is right – there is a fundamental change in the animal's behaviour. One day the dog is happy and eating, and the next day it is vacant, standing around staring. Provided the dog is still a companion, provided there is still a little soul there that you can relate to, well and good; these are all positive signs. But obviously if there is incurable pain and suffering, there's no way *that* should be allowed to continue, and we as a profession have the *privilege* to perform euthanasia because it is illegal to let dogs suffer, whereas humans have to drag on a bit. We are releasing the dog's soul from a life of anguish and agony, and it is incumbent upon everyone – the veterinary surgeon, the nurse and the owner – to make it as easy for the dog as possible, and not make a big thing of it. It has got to be a routine procedure. I will perform euthanasia with the client present, unless the client is so desperately upset that the dog is going to be upset.'

Avoid humane societies or anywhere else using electrocution or chloroform; of the electrothanator, Tony Cowie says, 'I'd rather use a twelve-bore shotgun.' The best method is an overdose of anaesthetic administered intravenously by the dog's regular vet, either at the surgery or at home – most vets will be willing to perform this special service on a home visit. Steel yourself, if you possibly can, to stay with your dog for the short time it takes, and be light and cheerful in your manner. It is quite painless and is usually over before the injection is complete. For a particularly nervous dog, it is possible to give a sedative beforehand to make him dozy for the injection. There's nothing to fear: to the dog, it's just another vaccination. The more you love this dog, the more you owe it to him to be cheerful in his last moments. Cry after he's gone, but comfort him now. Anything else is pure selfishness. Try to be business-like for five minutes; be an actor. Sign the release slip giving the vet permission to perform the euthanasia; this is not a heartless formality but a protection against misrepresentation, because cruel people have been known to take a neighbour's dog to be put down, and vets have been attacked and threatened with legal revenge by the rightful owner.

Vets on both sides of the Atlantic are very concerned about

human grief over euthanasia; one recently felt compelled to write a book[2] after a suicide attempt by the owner of a pet that had been put out of its misery, and there is an increasing awareness and sympathy among the veterinary profession who once used to politely push inconsolable owners out of the door. In the United States there are now veterinary counsellors to deal with this particular crisis, and soon there will be some in the UK. Don't let anyone at home or at work dismiss your feelings by saying, 'Oh, it was just a dog.' You tell them. It will make you feel better. There is nothing 'sentimental' or abnormal about grieving over a friend you've known intimately for perhaps ten to fifteen years. Sir Walter Scott, Lord Byron and some very tough men have been completely broken up by the death of a beloved dog, and one American couple told their counsellor, 'When we walk through the door, the house is so empty. It hurts. We want to know how long it's going to be like this. Are we going crazy?' They're not. It's natural. What to do about the pain and sorrow, though, is another matter.

There are one or two practical things to consider. Firstly, although the vet will dispose of animal patients' remains if you want, a decent burial for your dog, either in the garden or a pet cemetery, may give you a little comfort. The Queen's dear dogs are buried when they die beneath memorial tablets in the grounds of Sandringham. There is now also an increasing number of pet crematoria in Britain and the United States, such as the Cambridge Pet Crematorium, near Royston, Hertfordshire. Your own vet may be able to help you with local addresses, and this is something practical for you to do, to keep you from sorrowing away. The second thing is that, although all owners feel guilty about getting another dog – that somehow it wouldn't be 'fair' to their lost pet – it is none the less true that the best cure for deep mourning is to have something relying on you that you have to look after. There are thousands of mongrels desperate and literally dying for your love. Go along to a shelter while you're still blue and 'on the rebound', as lovers say, and have a look at them. This is not being 'unfaithful'. To know one mongrel is to care about them all, the whole poor, god-forsaken, mistreated race of them, and each one can only give its own devotion; it knows nothing of any rivalry in your heart. Experts and dog lovers alike advise you to get another dog fairly quickly before you harden your feelings. It isn't a replacement, so much as a therapy for you, and a kindness to the mongrel waiting to be rescued before it follows your own dog to the other world.

The last thing to consider is this: animals, like children, are much more knowing and wise about death than we are. Our intellects struggle against the injustice of it all; adults lose touch with nature, whereas children and dogs are still in tune with it. Dogs are 'psychic'; they have a 'sixth sense'. They can see ghosts, and *be* ghosts. They know about mysteries that we can only guess at, and I should like to end this book with a few 'spiritual tales' to illustrate the point.

Jilly Cooper's *Intelligent and Loyal* contains a number of intriguing stories about mongrels behaving strangely when their owners were dying, or very ill, or involved in traffic accidents. One started howling at the moment a favourite lady died 300 miles away; another sensed her mistress had had a car crash. Mongrels will often lift their heads and howl when someone absent dies, even though no one else in the house knows of the event. Jilly had many letters, too, about 'monghouls' – mongrel ghosties. One level-headed lady came home one day to find her deceased bitch Jen waiting at the door, and instinctively bent to stroke her before realizing she wasn't there, and other members of the family had similarly odd experiences of Jen about the house.

Nobel Prize-winner Konrad Lorenz was haunted by the footsteps of his dead dog Bully, and offers a scientific explanation to do with memory patterns. But the experience is very common. Misty images of dead pets have appeared in snapshots of other subjects; cases of canine apparition reported to the British College of Psychic Sciences in the 1920s include one from Lady Hehir, photographed with a wolf-hound, with a recently deceased cairn puppy curled up on the wolfhound's rump. Pythagoras, when a friend died, thought it a good idea to hold a dog near the mouth of the departed to receive his spirit, and the ancient Egyptians believed they were guided in the afterworld by the dog- or jackal-headed god Anubis.

Two cases of ghostbusting dogs were sent in to the old *Tailwagger* magazine (my thanks to Dr Alan Walker for bringing them to my attention). One concerned a couple living in a house formerly occupied by Judge Jeffreys. One night in the drawing-room, the family dog suddenly got up and started growling at some unseen presence in the corner. When his mistress became annoyed and dragged him by the collar towards the spot, he turned and bit her, which he had never done before. Another incident concerns the owner of a Sealyham terrier, who lay ill in bed after the death of his mother, with the dog by his side. 'Suddenly,' writes Mr Iredale, 'in the midst of my feeling of unutterable misery and loneliness, Trixie sat up as if called, and looked steadfastly – not at me – but at the empty chair by my bedside. Her behaviour was most remarkable. She pricked up her ears, wagged her tail, and wriggled with delight, pausing occasionally with head on one side as if listening carefully. Then she turned round to me and licked my face passionately, repeatedly transferring her gaze from me to the empty chair.'³

There are also, in the same magazine, two very intriguing stories of monghouls. The first comes from a London reader, reporting on a clairvoyant's messages, part of an investigation by the *Daily Sketch*. The medium Mrs Estelle Roberts, addressing a member of her audience, asked if she remembered a Mrs Mason, now departed, an old lady with a dog called Bennie, of whom she had been very fond. Bennie was eventually knocked down by a tram and killed. The message from the aforementioned Mrs Mason was that, 'when she got to the other side, she found Bennie, and his legs are all right.'⁴ The other dog tale has to do with the grandfather of a reader, a cleric in the East Riding of Yorkshire, who was on his way home in the dark with the missionary collections, when he was suddenly accosted by a strange and very large black dog of unidentifiable breed. The dog followed him, whining and occasionally growling softly, and licking the gentleman's hand as if it knew him and was trying to tell him something. A mile or so along the road, he caught sight of three heads, peering over a hedge, which moved as he moved along the deserted path. He realized that he'd been followed and was about to be set upon, but that the presence of the large dog, apparently his, seemed to deter the ruffians. Eventually they disappeared, but the dog accompanied him all the way to a well-lit toll-bar.

My grandfather was wondering what he would do with the dog, and to whom it belonged, for it was evidently miles from home – when all at once, it suddenly vanished. He stopped, whistled, called it, went back several hundred yards to look for it, but it was nowhere to be seen. It had disappeared as suddenly as it had come . . . Whatever others may say of their strange experiences, the above adventure really did happen. It occurred to my grandfather in the year 1855.[5]

Appendix 1
Blue Cross
Animal Welfare Services

Home finding is a major part of the work of the Animal Homes. All Blue Cross branches receive homeless and unwanted animals, as well as stray cats, and endeavour to find them good and caring homes. Two branches also receive stray dogs though these have by law to be first registered with the local police nearest to the place of finding – to give their owners a chance to trace them. All branches deal, too, with accident and emergency cases, including the rescue of trapped animals and strays. The branches provide 'welfare' boarding for the pets of pensioners, in cases of genuine need while in hospital or convalescing, and for other owners in emergency. Advice and help in an exceptionally wide circle of animal problems is always willingly given.

London services

The Blue Cross Hammersmith Hospital
Argyle Place, King Street, Hammersmith, London W6 0RQ
Telephone: 01-748 5150

The Blue Cross Victoria Animals Hospital
Hugh Street, Victoria, London SW1V 1QQ
Telephone: 01-834 4224

The Blue Cross Wandsworth & District Clinic, where a staff veterinary surgeon from the Victoria Hospital attends regularly.
483 Merton Road, Southfields, London, SW18 5LE
Telephone: 01-874 7310

The Society also has other local representatives and veterinary services in the London area.

Provincial services

Blue Cross Animal Centre
Wildmoor Lane, Wildmoor, Bromsgrove, Worcestershire, B61 0RS
Telephone: 021 453 3130

Blue Cross Field Centre
Home Close Farms, Shilton Road, Burford, Oxon, OX8 4PF
Telephone: 0993 823150

The Blue Cross Cambridge Animals Home, which has a general animal welfare service and specializes in the welfare of cats.
20 Garlic Row, Newmarket Road, Cambridge CB5 8HW
Telephone: 0223 350153

The Blue Cross Chalfont St Peter Animals Home
10 Grassingham End, Chalfont St Peter, Buckinghamshire SL9 0BP
Telephone: 0753 882560

The Blue Cross Dublin Branch, which provides Dublin with mobile animal clinics (with referral arrangements to a veterinary surgery for operations and special treatment) and horse ambulance services.
65 Annimo Road, Dublin 7, Eire
Telephone: 0001 43646

The Blue Cross Felixstowe Animals Home and Clinic
'Holly Cottage', 333 High Street, Walton, Felixstowe, Suffolk IP11 9QL.
Telephone: 0394 283254

Blue Cross Animals' Home
St Francis Fields of Rest for Horses, Morthiam, Sussex, TN31 6LP
Telephone: 07974 2243

The Blue Cross Grimsby Animals Hospital
207 Cleethorpe Road, Grimsby, South Humberside DN31 3BE
Telephone: 0472 42378

The Blue Cross Hertfordshire Dogs' Home, which receives stray dogs from the police, and also deals with cats, horses and other animals.
Kimpton Bottom, nr. Hitchin, Hertfordshire SG4 8EU
Telephone: 0438 832232

The Blue Cross Southampton Animals Home, which in addition to general welfare services receives stray dogs from the police.
Warren Avenue, Shirley, Southampton, Hampshire SO1 6AF
Telephone: 0703 771747

Blue Cross Animals' Home
Parklands, Station Road, Topcliffe, Thirsk, North Yorkshire, YO7 3SE
Telephone: 0845 577759

Blue Cross Animal Centre
Chilton Gate Kennels, Bickleigh, Tiverton, Devon, EX16 8RS
Telephone: 08845 291

All Blue Cross branches liaise with each other to ensure the best and speediest help for an animal.

Appendix 2
National Canine Defence League (NCDL)

Co. Antrim
Mrs J. Moore
Fairview, 60 Teeshan Road, Ballymena, Co. Antrim BT43 5PN
Telephone: Ballymena (0266) 652977

Berkshire
Mrs M. Iggleden
Plumbs Farm, Hamstead Marshall, Newbury, Berkshire RG15 0HR
Telephone: Kintbury (0488) 58391

Devon
Mrs P. Stow
Hazeldene, West Down, Ilfracombe, N. Devon EX34 8NU
Telephone: Braunton (0271) 812709

Dumfries
Mrs J. Coupland
Dovecotwells, By Glencaple, Dumfries DG1 4RH
Telephone: Glencaple (038777) 346

Mid Glamorgan
Mrs R. Day
Tondu Road, Bridgend, Mid Glamorgan CF31 4LH
Telephone: Bridgend (0656) 652771

Hampshire
Dr V. Gaybie
Farringdon Kennels, Farringdon, Nr Alton, Hampshire GU34 3NE
Telephone: Tisted (042058) 7225

Norfolk
Mr G.D. Good
North Farm Kennels, North End Road, Snetterton, Norfolk NR16 2LD
Telephone: Great Hockham (095382) 377

Shropshire
Mrs M. Thomas
Roden Lane Farm, Roden, Telford, Shropshire, TF6 6BP
Telephone: High Ercall (0952) 770 225

Sussex
Miss S. Prior
2–4 Robertson Road, Preston Park, Brighton, Sussex BN21 5NL
Telephone: Brighton (0273) 552764

Miss W. Farmer
Northbrook Kennels, Titmore Lane, Goring-by-Sea, Worthing, W. Sussex
Telephone: Worthing (0903) 504711

Warwickshire
Mrs J. Cashmore
Irelands Kennels, Honiley, Kenilworth, Warwicks. CV8 1NP
Telephone: Haseley Knob (092687) 398

Worcester
Mr G. Singleton
Heathercombe Lodge, Broadway Road, Wickhamford, Evesham, Hereford & Worcs.
Telephone: Evesham (0386) 830613

N. Yorkshire
Mrs A. Edwards
Brackenhill Kennels, Eskdale Side, Sleights, Whitby, N. Yorks
Telephone: Whitby (0947) 810380

W. Yorkshire
Mrs A. Sands
Adel Kennels, Eccup Lane, Adel, Leeds 16, W. Yorks
Telephone: Leeds (0532) 613194

Appendix 3
RSPCA Clinics

Headquarters' Hospitals and clinics

	Veterinary surgeon present	*First-aid and destructions*
Birmingham Birmingham Animal Hospital, Barnes Hill, Birmingham 29 5UP Tel: 021-426 6777	Mon–Fri: 9am–11am	Open 24 hours for emergencies

GREATER LONDON:

Camberwell 1 Station Road, SE5 9JJ Tel: 01-274 6995	Mon–Thurs: 2pm–3.30pm Fri: 10am–11.30am	Mon–Fri: 8.30am–1pm 2pm–5.30pm
Ealing and Hanwell 48 Uxbridge Road, W7 3PP Tel: 01-567 1839	Mon, Wed, Thurs: 11am–12 noon Fri: 2pm–3.30pm	Mon–Fri: 8.30am–1pm 2pm–5.30pm
Edmonton 79 Church Street, N9 9AA Tel: 01-807 3807	Mon: 2.30pm–3.30pm Tues, Thurs, Fri: 10am–11.30am	Mon–Fri: 8.30am–1pm 2pm–5pm
Fulham 8 Harwood Road, SW6 4PH Tel: 01-736 0833	Mon, Tues: 11am–12 noon Wed: 2.30pm–3.30pm Fri: 11.30–12.30pm	Mon–Fri: 8.30am–1pm 2pm–5.30pm

	Veterinary surgeon present	*First-aid and destructions*

Holloway
Harmsworth
  Memorial Hospital,
22 Sonderburg Road,
N7 7QD
Tel: 01–272 6214/5
	Mon–Fri:
	10am–11am
	2pm–3.30pm
		24-hour emergency
		  service

Kilburn 10 Cambridge Avenue, NW6 5AB Tel: 01–624 4610	Mon, Tues: 11am–12 noon Wed, Fri: 2pm–3.30pm	Mon–Fri: 8.30am–5.30pm
North Kensington 45 Bramley Road, W10 6SZ Tel: 01-969 5836	Mon: 9am–10.30am Tues: 2.30pm–3.30pm Thurs: 9am–10am	Mon–Fri: 8.30am–1.30pm 2pm–5pm

Putney
Putney Animal
  Hospital,
6 Clarendon Drive,
SW15 1AA
Tel: 01–789 8252
	Mon, Tues, Thurs:
	2pm–4pm
	Wed, Fri:
	10am–12 noon
		24-hour emergency
		  service

Southall The White House, Norwood Road, Southall, UB2 4JS Tel: 01-574 2710	Mon, Wed, Thurs: 9am–10am	Mon–Fri: 8.30am–1pm 2pm–5.30pm

Branch Clinics

Birmingham and District 179 Lea Hall Road, Glebe Farm, Birmingham 33	Mon, Wed: 2.30pm–3.15pm Fri: 11am–11.45am	As for treatments
Cradley Heath, Graingers Lane Tel: 0384 64868	Mon, Wed, Thurs: 11.am–11.45am	As for treatments
Russel Street, Wednesbury Tel: 021–556 3464	Mon, Wed, Thurs: 2.30pm–3.15pm	As for treatments

	Veterinary surgeon present	*First-aid and destructions*
356 Bearwood Road, Smethwick, Warley Tel: 021-429 3280	Tues: 9.15am–10am Thurs: 10am–10.45am	As for treatments

Bournemouth and District

144 Richmond Park Road, Bournemouth Tel: (0202) 526520	Mon, Thurs: 2pm–3pm	Mon–Fri: 9am–12.30pm 2pm–5pm

Cambridgeshire

Eddington Clinic, Great Eastern Street, Mill Road, Cambridge Tel: (0223) 247986	Tues, Thurs, Sat: 9am–10.30am	As for treatments

Cumbria (North and East)

8 West Walls, Carlisle Tel: (0228) 27152	Mon, Wed, Fri: 6pm–7pm	As for treatments

Enfield and District

45 Primrose Avenue, Enfield	Mon, Wed, Fri: 7.30pm–8.30pm	As for treatments

Essex (South), Southend and District

Chamberlain Avenue, Canvey Island	Wed: 2pm–3pm	As for treatments

Finchley, Golders Green, Hendon and District

Park Road, East Finchley, London N2	Wed: 5.30pm–6.30pm	As for treatments

Glamorgan (West) and Swansea

Charles Street, Neath Tel: (0639) 59395	Mon: 6.30pm–7.30pm	As for treatments

	Veterinary surgeon present	*First-aid and destructions*
Gloucester City and District		
Edwin Lea Clinic, 61 Horton Road, Gloucester	Tues: 10.45am–11.30am Thurs: 5.15pm–6pm	(Advice and destructions) Mon, Thurs, Fri: 9.45am–10.15am
Parrogate Road Cinderford Tel: (0594) 25294	Thurs: 4pm–4.30pm	(Advice and destructions) Mon, Thurs: 5pm–5.30pm
Gloucester (East) and Cheltenham		
2 Alleyne Lodge, Knapp Road, Cheltenham Tel: (0242) 570510	Wed: 6.30pm–7.30pm	Mon, Wed, Fri: 9am–10am
Great Yarmouth and District		
Tarworks Road, Great Yarmouth Tel: (0493) 858936	Tues, Fri: 6pm–7pm Mon, Sat: 9am–10am	As for treatments
Hampshire (Southampton and District)		
90 Northam Road, Southampton Tel: (0703) 23177	Tues, Thurs: 4pm–4.30pm	As for treatments
Harold Hill and Harold Wood		
Campbell Clinic, 144 Chippenham Road, Harold Hill, North Romford	Mon, Wed, Fri: 3pm–4pm	As for treatments
Kent (Ashford and District)		
34 Station Road, Ashford Tel: (0223) 21526	Tues, Fri: 3pm–4pm	As for treatments
Kent (Canterbury and District)		
21 Palace Street, Canterbury	Thurs: 6pm–6.45pm	As for treatments

	Veterinary surgeon present	First-aid and destructions
Kent (Folkestone and District) 21 Grace Hill, Folkestone Tel: (0303) 42592	Wed: 2.30pm–3.30pm	Mon, Thurs: 2.15pm–3pm
Kent (Mid, Maidstone and District) 72/74 Wheeler Street, Maidstone Tel: (0622) 675855	Wed: 2.30pm–3pm	As for treatments
Kent (North-West) 37 Gordon Road, Dartford	Tues: 3pm–4pm	As for treatments
158 Parrock Street, Gravesend	Thurs: 2.30pm–3.30pm	As for treatments
Kent (Tunbridge Wells and District) 136 Upper Grosvenor Road, Tunbridge Wells Tel: (0892) 23083	Wed: 5.30pm–6.15pm	Mon: 4pm–5pm Fri: 9.30am–10.30am
Kingston upon Thames and District 21 Orchard Road, Kingston upon Thames Tel: 01-546 3525	Tues, Fri: 2.30pm–3.30pm	As for treatments
Liverpool The Recreation Ground, Cherryfield Drive, Kirkby	Mon, Wed, Thurs: 11am–11.45am	Mon, Tues, Thurs: 10am–11am
Manchester and Salford 411 Eccles New Road, Salford 5 Tel: 061-736 6737	Mon, Fri: 10am–12 noon 2pm–4pm Sat: 9am–12 noon Mon, Wed, Fri: 5pm–7pm	As for treatments

	Veterinary surgeon present	First-aid and destructions
Poole and East Dorset		
60 Wimborne Road, Poole Tel: (0202) 674933	Tues, Fri: 2.30pm–3.30pm	Mon–Fri: 9am–1pm 2pm–5pm Sat: 9am–1pm
Preston and District		
196 Lancaster Road, Preston	Tues, Thurs: 7pm–8pm Sat: 12 noon–1pm	As for treatments
Slough, Uxbridge and District		
123 Uxbridge Road, Hillingdon Tel: Uxbridge (0895) 31435	Mon, Wed, Fri: 2.30pm–3.30pm	Tues: 8pm–9pm (Re-homing Tues and Sat)
68 Bath Road, Slough Tel: (0753) 25738	Mon: 2pm–3pm	Mon, Wed, Fri: 11am–12 noon Tues: 2.30pm–3.30pm Wed, Thurs: 7.30pm–8.30pm (Destructions Mon only)
Suffolk (East and Ipswich)		
35a St George's Street, Ipswich	Tues: 4.45pm–5.30pm Fri: 3.45pm–4.30pm	As for treatments
Surrey (Purley and District)		
New Addington Animal Clinic, Northdowns Road (Opposite Overbury Crescent), Purley	Tues: 7.15pm–8.15pm	Fri: 11am–12 noon

	Veterinary surgeon present	First-aid and destructions
Surrey (Sutton and District)		
302 High Street, Sutton	Wed, Fri: 2pm–3.30pm	Thurs: 2pm–3pm
Torquay and South-East Devon		
181 Union Street, Torquay Tel: (0803) 24253	Fri: 3.30pm–4.30pm	Mon–Fri: 9am–1pm 2pm–4.30pm Sat: 9am–12.30pm
Vale of Clwyd		
March Road, Rhyl Tel: (0745) 32150	Mon, Thurs: 3pm–4.30pm	As for treatments
Warrington and District		
Windmill Street, Delph Bridge, Runcorn	Thurs: 3.30pm–4pm	As for treatments
Wirral		
163 Livingstone Street, Birkenhead Tel: 051-652 1215	Mon, Wed: 4pm–4.30pm Fri: 3pm–3.30pm	As for treatments

Appendix 4
RSPCA Animal Homes (for Dogs)

HEADQUARTERS

RSPCA Millbrook Animal Centre
Millbrook Farm,
Guildford Road,
Chobham,
Surrey GU24 8ED
Tel: Chobham (099 05) 8792

RSPCA South Godstone Animal Centre
Elm Farm,
Water Lane,
South Godstone,
Surrey RH9 8JB
Tel: South Godstone (0342) 893117

RSPCA Southridge Animal Centre
Packhorse Lane,
Ridge,
Potters Bar,
Hertfordshire EN6 3LZ
Tel: Potters Bar (0707) 42153

BRANCH HOMES

Bath and District
Bath Animal Home,
The Avenue,
Claverton Down,
Bath,
Avon
Tel: Bath (0225) 66129

Birmingham and District
RSPCA Animal Home,
Barnes Hill,
Birmingham B29 5UP
Tel: 021-427 6111

Blackpool
RSPCA Longview Kennels,
Division Lane,
Marton,
Blackpool FY4 5EB
Tel: Blackpool (0253) 63991

Bournemouth and District, New Forest and Borough of Lymington, Poole and East Dorset
Hampshire and Dorset Animal Home,
Ashley Heath,
Ringwood,
Hampshire
Tel: Ringwood (042 54) 3896

Bristol and District
Bristol Dogs' Home and Clinic,
50 Albert Road,
St Phillips,
Bristol 2
Tel: Bristol (0272) 776043

Cardiff and District
RSPCA Animal Home,
Penarth Road,

Cardiff CF1 7TT
Tel: Cardiff (0222) 702352

Chester
RSPCA Kennels,
Gatehouse,
Greenbank,
Eaton Road,
Chester
Tel: Chester (0244) 675000

**Chesterfield and North
Derbyshire**
RSPCA Mayfield Kennels,
137 Spital Lane,
Chesterfield,
Derbyshire
Tel: Chesterfield (0246) 73358

Colwyn Bay and Aberconwy
RSPCA Animal Shelter,
Bryn-y-Maen,
Upper Colwyn Bay,
Clwyd
Tel: Colwyn Bay (0492) 2780

Coventry and District
RSPCA Kennels,
Brownshill Green Farm,
Northbrook Road,
Keresley,
Coventry
Tel: Keresley (020 333) 336616

Derbyshire (Derby and District)
RSPCA Kennels,
45 Abbey Street,
Derby
Tel: Derby (0332) 44620

Glamorgan (West) and Swansea
Swansea Dogs' Home,
Singleton Park,
Swansea
Tel: Swansea (0792) 203122

**Gloucester City and District and
Mid-Gloucestershire**
RSPCA Kennels,
c/o Farleigh Price Boarding
    Kennels,
Bristol Road,
Whitminster, Gloucester
Tel: Gloucester (0452) 740347

Gwent
RSPCA Animal Centre,
Ringland Way,
Ringland,
Llanwern,
nr. Newport
Tel: Llanwern (0633) 412049

Halifax and District
RSPCA Kennels and Clinic,
Wade Street,
Halifax,
Yorkshire HX1 1SN
Tel: Halifax (0422) 65628

Herefordshire
RSPCA Whitehouse Kennels,
Allensmore,
Hereford
Tel: Belmont (0432) 277503

Hull and East Riding
Hull and East Riding
    Animal Centre,
Clough Road,
Hull,
Humberside
Tel: Hull (0482) 41331/2

Isle of Wight
RSPCA Godshill Animal Centre,
Bohemia Corner,
Godshill
Tel: Godshill (0983) 840287

Lancashire (East)
RSPCA Animal Shelter,
Nearer Holker House Farm,
Altham,
Huncoat,
Lancashire
Tel: Accrington (0254) 31118

Leeds
RSPCA Animal Home and
    Clinic,
Cavendish Street,
Leeds LS3 1LY
Tel: Leeds (0532) 455132

**Leicester and South
Leicestershire**
RSPCA Woodside Animal
    Centre,
190 Scudamore Road,
Leicester LE3 1UQ
Tel: Leicester (0533) 877766/7

Liverpool
Horses' Rest, Dog's Home
    and Cats' Shelter
Higher Road,
Halewood,
Liverpool L26 9TX
Tel: 051-486 1706

Middlesex (North-West)
Mayhew Home,
Trenmar Gardens,
London NW10 6BJ
Tel: 01-969 0178

Newcastle upon Tyne
RSPCA Animal Centre,
Kyle Road,
Bensham,
Newcastle upon Tyne,
Tyne and Wear
Tel: Tyneside (091) 4604187

Norfolk (Mid) and Norwich
RSPCA Animal's Home,
143 Drayton Road,
Norwich
Tel: Norwich (0603) 46854

**Nottingham and
Nottinghamshire (East)**
Radcliffe-on-Trent Animal
    Shelter,
Nottingham Road,
Radcliffe-on-Trent
Tel: Radcliffe-on-Trent (060 73)
    4422

Nottinghamshire (West)
RSPCA Animal Centre,
c/o Baulker Lane Kennels,
Baulker Lane,
Clipstone,
Mansfield
Tel: Mansfield (0623) 26672

Oldham and District
RSPCA Kennels,
21a Rhodes Bank,
Oldham,
Lancashire OL1 1UA
Tel: 061-624 4725

Oxford
RSPCA Kennels,
c/o Ingleby Kennels,
Station Road,
Bletchington,
Oxford
Tel: Bletchington (0869) 50407

**Portsmouth and South-East
Hampshire**
RSPCA Animal Shelter,
346 Brook Lane,
Sarisbury Green,
Parkgate,
Southampton
Tel: Locks Heath (048 95) 5116

RSPCA Animal Home and
   Welfare Centre,
Regent Street,
Mile End,
Portsmouth
Tel: Portsmouth (0705) 823910

Preston and District
RSPCA Animals' Home,
Slack Cottage,
Longridge Road,
Preston,
Lancashire
Tel: Preston (0772) 792553

Rochdale
RSPCA Animal Home,
Red Cross Street,
Rochdale,
Lancashire OL12 0NZ
Tel: Rochdale (0706) 45000

Rotherham and District
RSPCA Animal Shelter,
Erskine Road,
Rotherham,
S. Yorkshire
Tel: Rotherham (0709) 363559

Scarborough and District
RSPCA Kennels,
c/o Wellfield Trekking Centre,
Staintondale Road,
Ravenscar
Tel: Scarborough (0723) 870182

Sheffield
Sheffield Animal Home,
83 Spring Street,
Sheffield 3
Tel: Sheffield (0742) 27542/3

Somerset (North)
RSPCA Animal Shelter,
172 Locking Road,
Weston-super-Mare

Tel: Weston-super-
Mare (0934) 27000

Somerset (South)
RSPCA Domestic Animal
   Centre,
Little Creech,
West Hatch,
Taunton TA3 5RT
Tel: Hatch Beauchamp (0823)
   480 384

**Southport, Birkdale and
District**
RSPCA Animal Home,
New Cut Lane,
Birkdale
Tel: Southport (0704) 67624

Staffordshire (North)
RSPCA Dogs' Home,
Sutherland Road,
Longton,
Stoke-on-Trent
Tel: Stoke-on-Trent (0782)
   313690

Suffolk (East) and Ipswich
RSPCA Animal Home,
2 Mill Lane,
Martlesham,
Woodbridge
Tel: Ipswich (0473) 623280

Sussex (Chichester and District)
RSPCA Animal Centre,
Mount Noddy,
Crocker Hill,
Eartham,
Chichester,
W. Sussex
Tel: Chichester (0243) 773359

Sussex (Mid) and Brighton
RSPCA Animal Centre,
London Road,

Patcham,
Brighton
Tel: Brighton (0273) 554218

Warrington and District
RSPCA Animal Centre,
Slutchers Lane,
Bank Quay,
Warrington
Tel: Warrington (0925) 32944

Wirral
Wallasey Dogs' Home,
Cross Lane,
Wallasey
Tel: 051-638 6318

Yorkshire (Bradford and
   District)
RSPCA Animal Home and

Clinic,
Mount Street (off Leeds Road),
Bradford 3
Tel: Bradford (0274) 23063

**Yorkshire (Doncaster and
District)**
RSPCA Animal Centre,
Black Firs Farm,
Doncaster Road,
Bawtry
Tel: Doncaster (0302) 710271

Yorkshire (York and District)
RSPCA Animals' Home and
   Clinic,
Landing Lane,
Clifton Road,
York
Tel: York (0904) 54949

Appendix 5
A Dogs' Home Directory

The following individual homes are mentioned in the text. Current information on local homes and shelters in the UK may best be obtained by telephoning your nearest RSPCA or NCDL branch. Small local shelters tend to be temporary; please check before making your journey.

The Dogs' Home, Battersea
4 Battersea Park Road, London SW8 4AA.
Telephone: 01-622 3626

The Birmingham Dogs' Home
New Bartholomew Street,
Digberth,
Birmingham B5 5QS
Telephone: (021) 643 5211

Ferne Animal Sanctuary (The Animal Defence Society Ltd)
Dogs now kennelled at:
The Margaret Green Foundation Trust,
Wool Lodge Kennels, Hyde, Nr. Bere Regis,
Nr. Wareham, Dorset.
Telephone: Bere Regis 471333

St Francis Charity For Stray Animals
Peppercorn Cottage, Water Street,
Berwick St. John, Nr. Shaftesbury, Dorset.
Telephone: Donhead 717

The Wood Green Animal Shelter
Kings Bush Farm, Godmanchester,
Nr. Huntingdon, Cambridgeshire.
Telephone: (0480) 830373

The Wood Green Animal Shelter
601 Lordship Lane, Wood Green,
London N22 5LG.
Telephone: 01-888 2351

The Wood Green Animal Shelter
Country Home, Heydon,
Nr. Royston, Hertfordshire.
Telephone: Royston (0763) 838329

Appendix 6
Useful Addresses

Ainsworths Homoeopathic
Pharmacy
38 New Cavendish Street,
London W1.
Telephone: 01-935 5330

British Union for the Abolition
of Vivisection
16A Crane Grove,
Islington,
London N7 8LB
Telephone: 01-607 1545/1892

Cadogan Gallery
15 Pont Street,
London SW1 9EH

Cambridge Pet Crematorium
Thriplow Heath,
nr. Royston,
Hertfordshire.

Dogs Monthly
Unit 8, New Road,
Ridgewood,
Uckfield,
East Sussex TN22 5SX.
Telephone: (0825) 5568

Hearing Dogs for the Deaf
Training Centre
2 Chinnor Hill,
Chinnor,
Oxon OX9 4BA.
Telephone: (0844) 53898

Nigel Hemming (oil and water
colourist)
38 Doctors Hill,
Pedmore,
Stourbridge,
West Midlands DY9 0YE.
Telephone: (0384) 379625

Herald Holiday Handbooks
18 High Street,
Paisley,
Renfrewshire PA1 2BX

Homoeopathic Development
Foundation
10A Cavendish Square,
London W1M 9AD.

International Fund for Animal
Welfare
Tubwell House, New Road,
Crowborough,
East Sussex TN6 2QH.
Telephone: (08926) 63374

Jenny Kearney's Grooming Pad
196 Bellenden Road,
Peckham, SE15.
Telephone: 01-732 3106

Jenny Kearney
East Lodge Grooming
Littlehampton Road,
Highdown,
Worthing
Telephone: (0903) 506435

The Kennel Club
1–4 Clarges Street,
Piccadilly,
London W1Y 8AB.
Telephone: 01-493 6651

Ministry of Agriculture,
Fisheries and Food
Hook Rise South,
Tolworth,
Surbiton,
Surrey KT6 7NF
Telephone: (0959) 34271

Roger Mugford, Animal
Behaviour Consultant,
10 Ottershaw Park,
Ottershaw,
Chertsey,
Surrey KT16 0QG
Telephone: (093287) 3625

The National Anti-Vivisection
Society Ltd
51 Harley Street,
London W1N 1DD.
Telephone: 01-580 4034

The National Canine Defence
League (HQ)
1 & 2 Pratt Mews,
London NW1 0AD.
Telephone: 01-388 0137

Our Dogs
Oxford Road Station Approach,
Manchester M60 1SX.

Telephone: 061-236 2660

The People's Dispensary for Sick
Animals (HQ)
PDSA House, South Street,
Dorking, Surrey RH4 2LB.
Telephone: (0306) 888291

PRO Dogs National Charity
Rocky Bank, 4 New Road,
Ditton, Maidstone, Kent
ME20 7AD.
Telephone: (0732) 848499

The Royal Society for the
Prevention of Cruelty to Animals
(HQ)
Causeway, Horsham,
West Sussex RH12 1HG.
Telephone: (0403) 64181

Scruffts/Hewitts Farm
Chelsfield,
Orpington,
Kent BR6 7QR.
Telephone: (0959) 34271

The Society for Companion
Animal Studies
Membership Secretary,
Mary F. Stewart DVM MRCVS,
University of Glasgow Veterinary
School,
Bearsden Road, Bearsden,
Glasgow G61 1QH.
Telephone: 041-942 2301

Notes

1 The true dog

1 Juliet Jewel, *Domesticated Animals from Early Times*, Heinemann/ BMNH, 1981, p. 37.

2 'Observations on the Pariah Dog', in *The Book of the Dog*, ed. Brian Vesey-Fitzgerald, Borden Publishing, Toronto, 1948, pp. 968– 990.

3 Miriam Rothschild, *Dear Lord Rothschild*, Hutchinson, 1983, p. 206.

4 Michael W. Fox, *The Dog: Its Domestication and Behaviour*, Garland STPM Press, 1978, p. 1.

5 Department of the Environment, 'Report of the Working Party on Dogs', HMSO, 1976, 14.2, 14.3, 14.5.

6 Charles Dickens, *All the Year Round*, 2 August 1862.

7 Michael W. Fox, *op. cit.*, p. 243.

8 John C. McLoughlin, *The Canine Clan*, Viking Press (NY), 1983, p. 139.

9 Edward C. Ash, *This Doggie Business*, Hutchinson, 1934, p. 31.

10 Major Harding Cox, *Dogs and I*, Hutchinson, 1923, p. xxiv.

11 Jewel, *op. cit.*, p. 45

12 Konrad Lorenz, *Man Meets Dog*, Penguin Books, 1953, pp. 87–9.

13 Michael Nelson, *A Pocket Book on Dog Care and Training*, Octopus, 1982, p. 5.

14 David Coffey, *A Veterinary Surgeon's Guide to Dogs*, World's Work, 1980, p. 29.

15 Erik Zimen, *The Wolf: His Place in the Natural World*, Souvenir Press, 1981, p. 34.

16 Letter to the author.

17 Letter to the author.

2 Acquiring a mongrel

1 Letter from Clive Hollands, *Veterinary Record*, 113,628 (24/31 December 1983).
2 Survey in R. C. G. Hancock, *The Right Way to Keep Dogs*, Elliot Right Way Books, revised ed. 1983, p. 25.
3 Pet Health Council information leaflet on canine parvovirus.
4 Catherine Fisher, *The Pan Book of Dogs*, Pan Books, 1958, reprinted 1969, p. 193.
5 David Taylor, *The Dog*, Unwin Paperbacks, 1980, p. 12.
6 Personal interview.
7 Jilly Cooper, *Intelligent and Loyal: A Celebration of the Mongrel*, Eyre Methuen, 1981, p. 27.
8 Personal interview.
9 Personal interview.

3 Visiting the shelters

1 Letter to *Dogs Monthly* magazine, 3 August 1983.
2 *All the Year Round*, 2 August 1862.

4 How to have a homebody

1 See, for example, the savage wolf 'status' fights in Erik Zimen's study, *The Wolf: His Place in the Natural World*, Souvenir Press, 1981.
2 If you would like to buy a Halti, or simply find out how it works, write to Dr Roger Mugford, 10 Ottershaw Park, Ottershaw, Chertsey, Surrey KT16 0QG.
3 David Coffey, *A Veterinary Surgeon's Guide to Dogs*, World's Work, 1980, p. 42.

5 Exercise, health and care

1 *Daily Mail*, 22 September 1984.
2 *Statistics of experiments on living animals, Great Britain 1983*, HMSO Cmnd. 9311, p. 14.
3 *Doncaster Advertiser, 20 March 1981*.
4 R. C. G. Hancock, *The Right Way to Keep Dogs*, Elliot Right Way Books, revised ed. 1983, p. 41.
5 Alan Walker, *Fit for a Dog: A Practical Guide to Feeding Dogs*, Davis-Poynter, 1980, p. 21. Dr Walker is a scientist and pet-food researcher.
6 Trevor Turner, *Know Your Dog: The Guide to Dog Care*, World's Work/Ventura Publishing, 1982, p. 14. Veterinary surgeon Trevor Turner is principal of a small-animal hospital.

7   Michael Nelson, *A Pocket Book on Dog Care and Training*, Octopus Books, 1982, p. 30. Michael Nelson is a veterinary surgeon.

6   Mongrel behaviour

1   Michael W. Fox, *The Dog: Its domestication and behaviour*, Garland STPM Press, 1978, p. 48.
2   David Taylor, *The Dog*, Unwin Paperbacks, 1980, p. 21.
3   Fox, *op. cit.*, pp. 54–5.
4   See, for example, Erik Zimen's studies in *The Wolf*, Souvenir Press, 1981.
5   Konrad Most, *Training Dogs*, Popular Dogs, 1962 ed., pp. 28–9.

8   Limelight and mongrels

1   Konrad Lorenz, *Man Meets Dog*, Penguin Books, 1953, p. 86.
2   Quoted in Gloria Cottesloe, *The Story of Battersea Dogs' Home*, David & Charles, 1979, p. 139.
3   Interview with Andrew Brace, *Dogs Monthly*, April 1983.
4   Jilly Cooper, *Intelligent and Loyal: A Celebration of the Mongrel*, Eyre Methuen, 1981, p. 2.
5   Interview in *You* magazine, *Mail on Sunday*, 9 September 1984.
6   Gloria Cottesloe, *op. cit.*, p. 132.
7   *Daily Mail*, 16 May 1983.

9   Mongrel service

1   *You* magazine, *Mail on Sunday*, 9 September 1984.
2   Published by Victor Gollancz Ltd, 1981.
3   *NCDL News*, spring 1983.
4   Dean Leo Bustad, former Professor of Veterinary Medicine, Washington State University.

10   From homes and abroad

1   *Daily Mail*, 13 February 1984.
2   *Daily Mail*, 10 September 1984.

12   The vale of years

1   David Taylor, *The Dog*, Unwin Paperbacks, 1980, p. 57.
2   Bruce Fogle, *Pets and Their People*, Collins, 1983.
3   *Tailwagger* magazine, August 1936.
4   *Ibid.*, January 1936.
5   *Ibid.*, April 1936.

Index